Critical Acclaim

Impeccably researched. Professor Charles Larson's book is elegantly written and, in my opinion, a must for everyone interested in African literature.

Nuruddin Farah

The scope and magnificence of writing from Africa in the last half century will perhaps surprise readers. This book is a brave attempt to convey something of the literary treasures of a much misunderstood continent.

Doris Lessing

A bold and daring documentation of decades of gruesome experiences on the part of African writers trying to break into print. Larson exposes the subtle and sometimes overt exploitation by some Western publishers of the dearth of well-established indigenous African publishing. He proposes far-reaching measures to improve not only the lot of present and future African writers, but also the structure and operations of the African book industry and indigenous publishing in Africa.

The proposals are made with compassion by a scholar who has actively followed and promoted literary development in Africa for over four decades. That the book is written by a non-African only reinforces its integrity and seriousness of purpose.

Ernest N. Emenyonu, St Augustine's College, North Carolina

After a long hiatus since his classic, albeit controversial work, *The Emergence of African Fiction* (1972), Charles R. Larson, a long respected figure in the criticism of African literature, has returned to this subject. This time his concern is not just the African literary text but the difficult circumstances of its creator. Written in a popular style, this book will appeal to lay people and specialists. Undoubtedly an important book, packed with revealing surprises, and to be recommended to anyone concerned about the literary face of the African continent.

Tijan M. Sallah

About the Author

Charles R. Larson is Professor of Literature at the American University, Washington, DC. In addition to several works of fiction of his own, he has specialized in the study of English-language creative writing by authors who may be considered to be outside the mainstream of North American and British fiction. For nearly forty years he has written hundreds of articles, reviews, essays and stories published in major magazines, as well as the following works of non-fiction:

The Emergence of African Fiction (1972)
The Novel in the Third World (1978)
American Indian Fiction (1978)
Invisible Darkness: Jean Toomer and Nella Larsen (1993)
Under African Skies: Modern African Stories (1997)

. . . .

The Ordeal of the African Writer

Charles R. Larson

. . . .

Zed Books
LONDON AND NEW YORK

For Roberta, Joshua, and Vanessa

The Ordeal of the African Writer was first published by Zed Books Ltd, 7 Cynthia Street, London N1 9JF, UK and Room 400, 175 Fifth Avenue, New York, NY 10010, USA in 2001.

Distributed in the USA exclusively by Palgrave, a division of St Martin's Press, LLC, 175 Fifth Avenue, New York, NY 10010, USA

Cover designed by Andrew Corbett
Set in Monotype Dante by Ewan Smith, London
Printed and bound in Malaysia

A catalogue record for this book is available from the British Library.

Library of Congress Cataloging-in-Publication Data

Larson, Charles R.
     The ordeal of the African writer / Charles R. Larson.
          p.   cm.
     Includes bibliographical references and index.
     ISBN 1-85649-930-8 – ISBN 1-85649-931-6 (pbk.)
     1. African literature (English)—History and criticism. 2. Literature and society—Africa—History. 3. Authorship—Social aspects—Africa. 4. Authors and publishers—Africa—History. 5. Publishers and publishing—Africa. 6. Politics and literature—Africa—History. I. Title

PR9340.L37 2001
820.9'896–dc21

                                                00-043476

ISBN 1 85649 930 8 cased
ISBN 1 85649 931 6 limp

Contents

Preface

My first exposure to African writers was in the summer of 1962 when I was undergoing training for teaching in Nigeria as a Peace Corps Volunteer. As I read Amos Tutuola's *The Palm-Wine Drinkard* (1952) and Chinua Achebe's *Things Fall Apart* (1958), I was immediately drawn into the extraordinary worlds of these narratives that were unlike anything else I had read during my education (which included a BA and an MA in English literature). During the two years I taught in Eastern Nigeria, I devoured as much African literature as I could get my hands on, including the 'novels' of the nearby Onitsha pamphleteers. By the time I returned to the United States in late 1964, I was excited enough about this writing to know that I wanted to devote my life to it.

I taught a course in 'African Literature' at the University of Colorado during the 1964–65 academic year, but because of the difficulty acquiring titles, half of the books were written not by Africans but by Europeans (Joseph Conrad, Graham Greene, Joyce Cary). The larger problem was attempting to convince American publishers to bring out US editions of the emerging African writers who were mostly being published in the UK and France. It was a long haul, and not very successful at the beginning.

The resistance that I encountered from publishers was mirrored in academe, still narrow-mindedly focused on the West. It took years to convince American faculties that African literature was worthy of study. Fortunately, there were academics open-minded enough to take the challenge along with me, though it proved difficult to find a director for my dissertation on African writers. The dissertation became a book, *The Emergence of African Fiction* (1972), one of the first critical examinations of African literature.

Thirty-plus years later, few literary scholars would deny the legitimacy of African literature. Nevertheless, this book is about the problems that African writers (in spite of the numerous prestigious awards many of them have received) still encounter when they attempt to become just that – African writers. The obstacles have hardly changed in the last half century, which is only to say that becoming a writer in Africa involves overcoming challenges and negotiating pitfalls rarely encountered by writers in the West. And yet, many western writers are unaware of the problems faced by writers in Africa (and in many parts of the so-called Third World).

The career of Amos Tutuola (and the publication of his novel, *The Palm-Wine Drinkard*) provides a striking example of a writer renowned in the West but largely ignored by his own people – a situation familiar to many of the writers who followed him. The Nigerian novelist, whom some critics today herald as one of the fathers of Magic Realism, experienced a life of frustration and obscurity; at his death in 1997, a collection had to be taken up to pay for his funeral.

The issues of which language to employ (African or European), of literacy and audience (50 per cent of the people on the continent cannot read), of economics (books are so expensive that few Africans can afford to purchase them), of an inadequate number of publishing outlets on the continent – all these are problems that still confront African writers today. In addition, they may encounter a second wall of obstacles: censorship, imprisonment, exile and worse.

Major portions of this book have been based on responses by African writers (published and unpublished) to a questionnaire I devised. The questionnaire stated the following:

> For a book about the African writer, I request narrative accounts of writers, describing their successes or failures in publishing.
>
> Individual chapters in this book will address questions of literacy, audience (who reads African literature? for what audience[s] is it written?), aesthetics (critical judgements from non-African readers who may not understand a writer's intent), issues of censorship, self-publishing as well as publishing with established publishing houses (both on and off the continent), as well as related issues of exile and alienation.
>
> Anecdotal information concerning any of these topics (and others you may want to propose) is welcomed.

Once these responses began to arrive, I realized that another questionnaire was needed so that African publishers could tell their side of the story.

In addition to those African writers, critics, educators and publishers who responded to my questionnaires and answered many additional questions, this book could not have been written without the invaluable assistance of Bernth Lindfors, Ernest Emenyonu and James Gibbs. These three critics of African literature patiently answered my frenzied questions about where I could locate a writer, what was that title to a work by a given writer I had forgotten, and where additional sources could be found for many of the areas covered in this book. Lindfors and Emenyonu also served as invaluable first readers for sections of the manuscript as it developed, as did Tijan M. Sallah.

Additionally, the following people aided me in my research, often by relating their experiences with publishing: Cyprian Ekwensi, Similih M. Cordor, Elinor Sisulu, Véronique Tadjo, Yvonne Vera, especially; but also Kehbuma Langmia, F. Odum Balogum, Douglas O. Temile, Mzamane Nhlapo, William Saidi, Irene Staunton, Mwamba Cabakulu, Jare Ajayi, Taban lo Liyong, Lenrie Peters, Ngugi wa Thiong'o, Chinua Achebe, Tijan M. Sallah, Steve Chimombo, Sindiwe Magona, Nuruddin Farah, Jekwu Ikeme, Wole Soyinka, Niyi Osundare, Tess Onwueme, Margaret Ling, Trish Mbanga, Miriam Bamhare, Terence Ranger, Nevilles Bsquared Oguohwo, Sanya Osha, Louis-Marie Ongoum, N. Cabakulu, Stephen Gray, George Ngwane, Segun Ourowaiye, Henry Chakava, James Tumusiime, Manthia Diawara, Neely Tucker, Gilbert Doho, Joop Berkhout, Muthui Kiboi, B. Sodindwa Neube, Hans Zell, Colin McGee, Aminata Sy, Buma Kor, Madieyna Ndiaye, Lupenga Mphande, Jeremy Ng'aug'a, Becky Clarke. To anyone else I may have forgotten – I apologize.

Finally, this book is my own modest praise-song to contemporary African writers, still walking proudly in the footsteps of their traditional storytellers, their griots, in spite of impossible odds.

. . . .

CHAPTER I

The Example of Amos Tutuola: Accidental Artist or Really Writer?

[W]hen it was the 6th month after my father had died, the tapster went to the palm-tree farm on a Sunday evening to tap palm-wine for me. When he reached the farm, he climbed one of the tallest palm-trees in the farm to tap palm-wine but as he was tapping on, he fell down unexpectedly and died at the foot of the palm-tree as a result of injuries. As I was waiting for him to bring the palm-wine, when I saw that he did not return in time, because he was not keeping me long like that before, then I called two of my friends to accompany me to the farm. When we reached the farm, we began to look at every palm-tree, after a while we found him under the palm-tree, where he fell down and died. (Amos Tutuola, *The Palm-Wine Drinkard*, 1952)

I went to the Labour Department later, to get him to sign my copy of his book, and found him sitting in a corner in his loose-fitting uniform, asleep. I had to get to him past row on row of bespectacled Nigerians, sitting at their desks in bureaucratic self-satisfaction and palpably annoyed at the breach of decorum in a white man's calling on a messenger. He asked me what I wanted him to write and then, after signing the inscription, he said: 'I think, when you reach there, the U.S.A., you write a letter to me.' I said I would, but why did he want me to? 'So I know you not forget me.' (Eric Larrabee, Review of *The Palm-Wine Drinkard*, *The Reporter*, 12 May 1953)

§ PURISTS disagree about the precise date for the birth of modern African fiction, but if Anglophone writing south of the Sahara is mentioned, then the publication of Amos Tutuola's *The Palm-Wine Drinkard* is the date most often cited. (Narratives by several earlier black writers never achieved the exposure of Tutuola's novel.) Published by Faber and Faber in England in 1952, *The Palm-Wine Drinkard* was reprinted in the United States by Grove Press the following year. By that time, the hoopla had already begun and the controversy continued, largely unabated, until the author's death in 1997.

Amos Tutuola was born in 1920, in Abeokuta in Western Nigeria, in what is frequently identified as one of the centres of Yoruba culture. His formal education began in 1934 at the local Salvation Army School and subsequently continued, through the aid of a patron (a civil servant named F. O. Mornu), two years later in Lagos. By the author's own account, he was a quick-witted student, twice given special promotions (skipping a year), yet he was hampered not by his own intellectual capabilities but by external circumstances over which he had little control.

F. O. Mornu's housekeeper sent the young student off to Lagos High School each day without breakfast or money for lunch, apparently pocketing the money herself. She expected him to survive on one meagre meal a day when he returned home from school in the afternoon. In 'My Life and Activities', included as an afterword to the American edition of *The Palm-Wine Drinkard*, Tutuola describes this woman as 'cruel-hearted' (p. 126) and 'hard-hearted' (p. 127). Furthermore, the boy was afraid to complain to his benefactor about his ill-treatment for fear that Mornu would cease paying his school fees. When he returned to Abeokuta after a little more than a year, Tutuola decided to remain at home instead of returning to the coldhearted housekeeper.

Tutuola's father was a poor farmer, but he was nevertheless able to pay the fees for the Anglican Central School, as he had earlier when the boy lived in Abeokuta. These studies ended in 1939 when Tutuola's father died and no one else could pay the tuition. Thus, his education was limited to six years of frequently interrupted study, after which he worked at the family farm for a year before returning to Lagos where he lived with a half-brother and began learning smithery. In the author's own words: 'Having qualified for this trade, I struggled and joined the W. African Air Corps (RAF) in the year 1944, as a Coppersmith, as blacksmithing also pertains to this trade. My rank is AAI, and the number is WA/8624' (p. 129). These dates have been disputed by scholars. At the end of the Second World War,

Tutuola attempted a number of unsuccessful business ventures, including setting up his own blacksmith shop.

Employment was particularly difficult because of the number of Nigerian soldiers returning from overseas, so Tutuola became a messenger in the Department of Labour in Lagos. It was there, during the long hours when he had little to do, that he began writing down the Yoruba tales he had heard from his mother and from others as a child. As he stated in the concluding sentence of 'My Life and Activities': 'it was hard for me before I obtained this unsatisfactory job which I am still carrying on at present' (p. 130).

The handwritten manuscript for *The Palm-Wine Drinkard* – which Tutuola later claimed was written in a two-day explosion of creativity (and subsequently revised over several months) – was initially sent to the United Society for Christian Literature in London. Tutuola had seen an advertisement in *Nigeria Magazine* describing the society's publications by African authors, brought out by their publishing division, the Lutterworth Press. The author's education had been Christian; publishing in Nigeria was close to non-existent. Fortunately, although they would not publish it themselves, the Lutterworth editors were able to recognize the significance of Tutuola's imaginative narrative and eventually sent it to Faber and Faber after failing to interest another publisher who had responded negatively with the statement, 'Don't be silly!' (see Lindfors, 'Amos Tutuola's Search', *Journal of Commonwealth Literature*, 1982). After significant editing, Tutuola's novel was published in 1952, although it may have been written as early as three years before that.

The controversy began almost immediately.

Reviewers were largely divided into two factions: English and American critics were captivated, enthralled by Tutuola's exotic story as well as his style; African critics, however, were made uncomfortable by a fear that westerners would regard Tutuola as a 'typical educated African'. It was a delicate time in the history of colonization in Africa. Demobilization had returned thousands of African soldiers to their homelands, men who, in concert with African leaders, were beginning to argue more vocally for independence from the colonial powers. In his memorial for Tutuola in 1997, Ernest Emenyonu wrote: 'the best of African politicians educated in some of the best universities in Europe and America, would present the case for their country's independence and debate it flawlessly in the imperialist's own language, on his own soil' ('In Memoriam: Amos Tutuola', p. 3). Amos Tutuola did not employ the Queen's English.

It is difficult to say whether it was the language or the story that most impressed the western critics of Tutuola's narrative. The Welsh poet Dylan Thomas began his review in *The Observer* (6 July 1952) by announcing: 'This is the brief, thronged, grisly and bewitching story, or series of stories, written in young English by a West African, about the journey of an expert and devoted palm-wine drinkard through a nightmare of indescribable adventures, all simply and carefully described in the spirit-bristling bush.' Three paragraphs later, after describing some of the extremes of the story, Thomas concluded: 'The writing is nearly always terse and direct, strong, wry, flat and savoury; the big, and often comic, terrors are as near and understandable as the numerous small details of price, size, and number; and nothing is too prodigious or too trivial to put down in this tall, devilish story.'

One wonders what would have been the fate of *The Palm-Wine Drinkard* without the extraordinary good fortune of Thomas's critique. Indeed, Bernth Lindfors has written: 'Tutuola may owe much of his early notoriety to the endorsement of the famous Welsh poet' (*Critical Perspectives*, 1975, p. 3). Subsequent printings of and advertisements for Tutuola's work, including the first American edition, have usually quoted from the Dylan Thomas review, which set the tenor for many of the responses that were to follow.

Months later in *The Listener* (13 November 1952), Arthur Calder-Marshall echoed the Thomas review, referring to Tutuola's narrative as 'a very curious work ... this herald of the dawn of Nigerian literature.' The following year, American reviewers highlighted Tutuola's language. Eric Larrabee, in *The Reporter* (12 May 1953), described the book as 'written in English but not an English of this world', and Selden Rodman in the *New York Times Book Review* (20 September 1953) went a step further by calling the author: 'a true primitive', and the work itself 'naive poetry'. Anthony West in *The New Yorker* (5 December 1953) carried the critical argument even further by describing Tutuola's style as 'naive and barbaric'. He noted: 'One catches a glimpse of the very beginning of literature.' Variants on these statements appeared in other critical responses, as well as in V. S.

Pritchett's review of Tutuola's second book, *My Life in the Bush of Ghosts*, first published in 1953: 'One cannot tell whether works like Tutuola's are freaks that mark a linguistic crisis or rebirth in a culture … Tutuola's voice is like the beginning of man on earth, emerging, wounded and growing.' Scratch the surface of these statements and we find disturbing parallels to Joseph Conrad's *Heart of Darkness*: 'Going up that river was like travelling back to the earliest beginnings of the world … '; 'We were wanderers on prehistoric earth, on an earth that wore the aspect of an unknown planet … in the night of first ages' (pp. 30, 32). For West African critics and readers of Tutuola's narrative, comments such as those by West and Pritchett smacked of the cult of the primitive, and everyone knew where the heart of darkness was located. Chinua Achebe had yet to publish *Things Fall Apart* (1958) and was years from writing about Conrad's racism, yet Africans responding to *The Palm-Wine Drinkard* were anything but comfortable with what they had read and unsure whether their hostility should be directed at the author, his highly touted narrative, or his publisher.

In *Critical Perspectives on Amos Tutuola* (1975), Bernth Lindfors, the editor, refers to the African response to Amos Tutuola's first two novels as 'the controversy in *West Africa*', perhaps with no pun intended. *West Africa* was edited and printed in London, though its contents covered the area designated by its name. Not all of the voices in the controversy were African; some were Europeans with first-hand experience of the continent. The attacks on the writer concerned not only his linguistic skills but also his originality, though under both these reservations lay the growing dismay that Tutuola, with his skimpy education and no more than a basic use of English, had garnered attention that did not enhance the image of Africans in the eyes of westerners. The 'African' commentators were fairly negative, unwilling to praise an African original. A basic dispute about aesthetics was emerging here, which would take on interesting permutations among subsequent generations of African writers and their international critics.

In *West Africa* on 27 February 1954, Eric Robinson paved the way for the controversy by decrying Tutuola's linguistic skills: 'Mr. Tutuola's English is a very unreliable instrument but it has a gusto, and there can be no question that the stories come over with a greater pungency in his two books than if his English had been "correct" but lifeless.' Two months later, in a letter to the same publication (10 April), Babasola Johnson claimed that *The Palm-Wine Drinkard*:

> ... should not have been published at all. The language in which it is written is foreign to West Africans and English people, or anybody for that matter. It is bad enough to attempt an African narrative in 'good English', it is worse to attempt it in Mr. Tutuola's strange lingo (or, shall I say, the language of the 'Deads'?). The language is not West African Patois as some think. Patois is more orderly and intelligible than the language of *The Palm-Wine Drinkard*. Patois does not contain such words as 'unreturnable', 'weird' or such expressions as 'the really road'.

Tutuola as a writer may be *sui generis*, yet the same is true of some of his most celebrated predecessors who also 'violated' the presumed purity of the English language. Take James Joyce and William Faulkner as prime English and American examples. Would Dylan Thomas have been so exuberant about *The Palm-Wine Drinkard* if the language were standard English?

Worse, little credit was granted to the writer for his story (or stories) itself. Eric Robinson also found fault with the author's storytelling: 'The book is firmly rooted in West African folk-lore; a number of the stories can be identified in the recent Penguin edition of West African folk tales. As Dr. Parrinder tells us in his introduction, the stories are "genuine African myths, such as are told in countless villages round the fire or in the tropical moonlight".' Worse, wasn't Tutuola indebted to the published narratives of Chief D. O. Fagunwa, written in Yoruba?[1]

Underlying all these attacks on the author's originality both as a storyteller and as an innovator with language was the uncomfortable issue of image. Tutuola must not serve as an example of African creativity, his compatriots suggested, because he did not have the

---

1. Chief D. O. Fagunwa (1910–63), popular Yoruba novelist, who began publishing in 1939. His first novel, *Ogboju ode ninu igbo Irunmale* (The Skilful Hunter in the Forest of Four Hundred Spirits), was followed by nearly a dozen others. Some critics accuse Tutuola of heavily relying on Fagunwa's writings.

proper academic (educational) credentials. How dare this upstart be considered as an artist. As I. Adeagbo Akinjogbin wrote in a letter to *West Africa* (5 June 1954), after confessing that he had read neither of Tutuola's books:

> Most Englishmen, and perhaps Frenchmen, are pleased to believe all sorts of fantastic tales about Africa, a continent of which they are profoundly ignorant. The 'extraordinary books' of Mr. Tutuola (which must undoubtedly contain some of the unbelievable things in our folklores) will just suit the temper of his European readers as they seem to confirm their concepts of Africa. No wonder then that they are being read not only in English, but in French as well.[2] And once this harm (I call it harm) is done, it can hardly be undone again. Mr. Tutuola will get his money and his world-wide fame all right, but the sufferers will be the unfortunate ones who have cause to come to England or Europe. I am not being unduly anxious.

The implication is that Akinjogbin suffered personal indignities because Europeans connected him with Amos Tutuola. No surprise, then, that he concludes that Amos Tutuola's books are of 'no literary value'.

What was this curious book that had inspired such a wide spectrum of responses?

Though *The Palm-Wine Drinkard* has similarities with medieval epics, romances and traditional quest narratives, in these postmodern days it is easiest simply to classify the work as a novel. There is a central plot, with ample development, conflict and resolution. Early readers and critics no doubt avoided categorization of Tutuola's story because of the episodic narrative and the unconventional hero narrator, both of which might also lead to the narrative's subclassification as picaresque. After the death of his palm-wine tapper, the hero (the Drinkard) attempts to locate his deceased supplier, encounters numerous obstacles that thwart his search, but eventually locates him in the afterworld (the domain of 'the Deads'). The dead Tapster, Baity, informs the Drinkard that he must remain in the world of the living, that alives cannot live with Deads; hence the Drinkard's

---

2. *The Palm-Wine Drinkard* had quickly been translated into French and several other languages.

return to his home with the accumulated wisdom of his lengthy journey.

The Palm-Wine Drinkard begins: 'I was a palm-wine drinkard since I was a boy of ten years of age. I had no other work more than to drink palm-wine in my life. In those days we did not know other money, except COWRIES, so that everything was very cheap, and my father was the richest man in our town' (p. 7). The young, alcoholic Drinkard tells us that he and his 'uncountable' friends were drinking 150 kegs of palm-wine each morning and another seventy-five every evening. But after the Tapster had been tapping palm-wine for the Drinkard for fifteen years, he 'fell down unexpectedly and died' (p. 8). The Drinkard's fickle friends stopped visiting him. The Drinkard states: 'then I thought within myself that old people were saying that the whole people who had died in this world, did not go to heaven directly, but they were living in one place somewhere in this world. So that I said that I would find out where my palm-wine tapster who had died was' (p. 9).

The encounter with the fantastic or the supernatural, as many initial readers regarded it, meant that Tutuola's narrative could not be called a novel. But now that Magic Realism is no longer regarded as the exclusive domain of writers of *El boom*, *The Palm-Wine Drinkard* looks more like a novel than ever before. Recently, scholars have even gone so far as to suggest that Tutuola is one of the fathers of Magic Realism.

Before he arrives at the world of the Deads, Tutuola's Drinkard encounters a series of curious creatures (both human and sub-human) who repeatedly test his prowess as a hero by throwing unexpected obstacles in his pathway. From many of these encounters, the Drinkard gains further experience and wisdom, in spite of the frustrating and frightful nature of many of the events. The plot, then, becomes a series of testings, of giving and taking, of learning and growing. One of the first of these is representative of many of the subsequent episodes: after several weeks of travel, the Drinkard arrives at a new village and is promised by one of its denizens that he will be informed where his Tapster is if, first, he will do what the villager requests of him. The task is to find the man's daughter and bring her back home. The Drinkard does this and is given the young woman as his wife.

That is the unembellished episode, which would be nothing

extraordinary without the wondrous world into which Tutuola has thrust his protagonist. The woman, or daughter, has disappeared after she followed a curious creature (or 'complete gentleman' [p. 18]) into the 'endless forest' (p. 19), having refused to marry the suitor her father had chosen for her. The Complete Gentleman's beauty is so extraordinary that 'if he had been an article or animal for sale, he would be sold at least for £2000' (p. 18). The Drinkard further states of this gentleman:

> if I were a lady, no doubt I would follow him to wherever he would go, and still as I was a man I would jealous him more than that, because if this gentleman went to the battle field, surely, enemy would not kill him or capture him and if bombers saw him in a town which was to be bombed, they would not throw bombs on his presence, and if they did throw it, the bomb itself would not explode until this gentleman would leave that town, because of his beauty. (p. 25)

By the time the Drinkard arrives on the scene, the Complete Gentleman has lost all of his beauty, which was borrowed. His arms, legs, belly, ribs, chest – even the skin on his head – were rented from other creatures. As the young woman follows him into the endless forest, the Complete Gentleman returns all of these borrowed parts to their owners, paying the rental money for them, and finally becoming nothing more than a disembodied skull. The woman had no power to stop following the transformed creature and becomes his captive in a house filled with other skulls. The Drinkard, who has magical powers of his own, transforms himself into air, and thus gains entry into the room where the woman is captive, eventually rescuing her – not without further complications and transformations of himself – and returns her to her father. The episode concludes with the Drinkard's statement: 'That was how I got a wife' (p. 31).

This celebrated episode from *The Palm-Wine Drinkard* exists in numerous versions in West African cultures, not simply in Tutuola's own Yoruba cosmology, and in many ways is representative of traditional teaching tales. The messages are obvious: obey your parents or you may encounter something worse than the life they have planned for you. Danger is often difficult to recognize. Do not be deceived by beauty which is only skin deep. Seemingly, the young woman learns her lesson, for she not only becomes the Drinkard's faithful wife, accompanying him throughout the rest of the narrative, but also aiding him in his numerous travails. It might also be noted that the Drinkard acquires his wife on one of the few occasions when someone else (the Drinkard's future father-in-law) demonstrates any true generosity.

It is almost impossible for anyone to read *The Palm-Wine Drinkard* without delight and amazement and a good bit of chuckling on the side. The Drinkard's encounters in the endless forest are suspenseful and hair-raising, inventive and resourceful. Tutuola has opened the doors of a magic kingdom no less amazing than those we encounter in the works of Gabriel Garcia Marquez, Isabel Allende and Salman Rushdie – to name only three subsequent writers whose imaginations are no less daring than Tutuola's.

At the same time, it must be stressed that the sub-text of Tutuola's story is not very far removed from much more seemingly realistic African novels. On one level, *The Palm-Wine Drinkard* relates the same story as Chinua Achebe's *Things Fall Apart* (1958): the breakdown of the traditional African order in response to the onslaught of what is new and different, that is, enormous cultural change. Achebe accomplishes this by describing what happens to an African village upon the arrival of the first Europeans, yet he also makes it quite clear that the traditional order had reached a critical state of self-examination because of cultural rigidities and inflexibilities that provided little room for deviation from the norm. Things fall apart, then, for two reasons: internal and external.

The traditional world described in *The Palm-Wine Drinkard* is as harsh and vindictive as Achebe's. It takes the Drinkard ten years to locate his dead Tapster, largely because the people he encounters along the way are not very helpful. As he tells us of one of the villages he visits, 'both adults and children were very cruel to humanbeings' (p. 58), but the same statement could be made of numerous other places he visits and people he meets on his journey. Simply put, the people the Drinkard asks for help are mean to him, nasty, even cruel. He is tortured, lied to and repeatedly tricked. Though he himself fulfils his side of numerous agreements, the people he encounters generally renege on their part of the bargain. Furthermore, the roads are unsafe for travel, populated with gangs of highwaymen and thugs, suggesting that traditional life has already fallen apart because of greed and self-centredness. Even in his own village, the Drinkard's so-called friends desert him once he can no longer supply them with unlimited amounts of palm-wine, implying that it may have been the loss of camaraderie as much as the Tapster's death that instigates the Drinkard's journey in the first place. At the end of the story, after the Drinkard returns home, he is the victim of further greed and meanness from his compatriots.

Most western critics responded enthusiastically to Tutuola's playful inventiveness with language. Tutuola took the English language and turned it upside-down, inventing new constructions and a new syntax, not so much out of ignorance (the lack of a formal education) as roughshod ownership. As a colonial subject, why couldn't he use the colonial masters' language in any way he wanted? To a certain extent, his writing at the time was like that of someone learning a new language and still making basic errors. What naïve painters with no formal training had done in art, Tutuola did with words. One thinks of the works of Grandma Moses or of Haitian paintings from the 1950s and 1960s that include too many arms and legs to match the torsos. Add a smattering of Hieronymus Bosch's macabre universe – the 400 dead babies the Drinkard and his wife encounter on one of the bush roads or the Tapster's training for two years before 'he had qualified as a full dead man' (p. 100) – and it becomes clear that Amos Tutuola's work is closely related to that of the naïve painters.

Tutuola's language is not so much West African Pidgin English, which has its own syntax and structure, as the writing of an inspired pupil whose exuberance has overtaken his command of basic grammar. Nor is it exactly the 'rotten English' that Ken Saro-Wiwa used in *Sozaboy* (1985). Close to automatic writing – if the first draft of *The Palm-Wine Drinkard* spilled out of the author in two days – no wonder it often seems uncorrected and unpolished. And therein lies much of the joy of his novel. The images are fresh and original (and definitely at odds with European models); both the story itself and the language are filled with hyperbole, unfathomable exaggeration, even surrealism (when the Drinkard passes through the door of the Faithful Mother's tree, he doesn't enter a delineated space but an entire new world). Distances of time and mathematical calculations defy western logic. Although foreign terms creep into his writing ('if bombs explode' [p.

45]; 'technicolours' [p. 68]; 'drinks and cigarettes' [p. 71]; 'as if a photographer was focusing somebody' [p. 65]), it is more frequently the charming expression that catches the eye: 'I thought within myself' (p. 9); 'his havocs and bad character' (p. 34); 'he himself was refuse' (p. 45); 'laugh was his profession and he was feeding on it' (p. 46); 'it was also a various bush' (p. 55); 'a really road' (p. 101). Add to these innovations the typographical emphasis of certain words, expressions, and summary passages scattered throughout the text –

> RETURN THE PARTS OF BODY TO THE
> OWNERS; OR HIRED PARTS OF THE
> COMPLETE GENTLEMAN'S BODY TO BE
> RETURNED (p. 19)

– and it is impossible not to regard Tutuola as a postmodern writer with few antecedents or authorities.

How did Tutuola himself respond to his fame (or his notoriety)? It might be more pertinent to ask: What was it like to be a writer in a society where there were no published writers? Eric Larrabee has described his encounter with Tutuola (see the epigraph to this chapter), seeking him out in the Nigerian Department of Labour in order to have the author inscribe his novel, and finding him asleep at his job. Bartleby? Was Larrabee's request the first that Tutuola had received to autograph a copy of his novel? Did his request that Larrabee should write him a letter 'So I know you not forget me' imply that Tutuola was already concerned that his new-found profession as a writer would lead to few changes in his life?

Partial answers to these questions are suggested by another passage from Larrabee's review of *The Palm-Wine Drinkard*, which states: 'As an exercise in imagination, try to conceive of an author who (1) probably has never met another author, (2) owns no books, (3) is not known to his daily acquaintances as an author, (4) has no personal contact with his publisher, (5) is not certain where his book is on sale, and (6) does not think of himself as an author.' There is an element of truth to all of these conditions, except for the one about owning books. Certainly, Tutuola knew the value of possessing books as intellectual property, and there is ample evidence that he had already acquired a personal library.

Probably, however, no one was more surprised by the notoriety of *The Palm-Wine Drinkard* than Tutuola himself, beginning with the novelty of becoming a writer. What would that have meant in Nigeria in 1952? So widespread was illiteracy that it is possible that none of Tutuola's closest friends or members of his extended family would have been able to read his book. Would his co-workers at the Department of Labour have responded differently? Chances are that their own literacy might be so minimal that they would not consider reading something as intimidating as a 'novel.' Added to that is the likelihood that the book, an imported object, if available at stationery outlets (since there were no genuine bookshops in the country at the time) would be beyond the reach of most people's salaries. In a 'Portrait' of the author that appeared in *West Africa* on 1 May 1954, the unidentified reporter states that the BBC had broadcast three of Tutuola's stories and that the author was considering taking 'evening classes to "improve" himself'. Yet he goes on to state: 'Very few Nigerians seem to have heard of Tutuola and fewer have read his books.'

Indeed, Tutola may have wondered why his life had changed so marginally after publishing his narrative. As a messenger in the Department of Labour, he received a salary of approximately £85 a year, not a paltry sum in 1952. The advance that he received from Faber and Faber was £25, equal to more than three months' salary, still a significant amount of money in Nigeria at the time.

Whether because of his increased income or something else, Tutuola was hopeful that his writing would change his life. According to Bernth Lindfors, writing in the *Journal of Commonwealth Literature* in 1982, eighty days after Faber and Faber published *The Palm-Wine Drinkard*, Tutuola sent them the manuscript for *My Life in the Bush of Ghosts*, which was not his second novel but actually his third. This curious fact about Tutuola's publishing career was not revealed at the time and is worth relating, since in many ways it sounds like a story the writer himself might have invented. It also illustrates many of the related impediments to becoming a writer in Africa that have persisted to this day.

In 1948 Amos Tutuola wrote a novel called *The Wild Hunter in the Bush of Ghosts*. Lindfors, who unravelled the story about this earlier work, has noted that Tutuola began writing it because 'he was very eager to find ways to supplement his income' ('Introduction', p. xi) after having recently married. While working in the Department of Labour, he had also set up a photo-service, hoping to become a professional photographer, and had ordered publications from the Focal Press in London.

When he finished writing *The Wild Hunter in the Bush of Ghosts*, Tutuola sent the Focal Press a letter about the manuscript which, he claimed, could be 'illustrated with photographs of the spirits' (p. xi). A. Kraszna-Krausz, the director of the Focal Press, recalled the incident many years later. How could anyone resist? The English already had a reputation for 'photographing fairies', as demonstrated by Arthur Conan Doyle and Charles Castle. Yet when Tutuola's seventy-seven-page handwritten manuscript arrived months later and the negatives submitted along with it were developed, they turned out to be 'snapshots of hand-drawn sketches of spirits and other phenomena featured in the story. Tutuola had hired a schoolboy to draw these illustrations and then had photographed them' (p. xii). The Focal Press 'bought' the manuscript and the photographs, with no intention of publishing them, paying Tutuola something in the region of £5 for his efforts, which, Lindfors speculates, 'may have seemed like manna from heaven to a messenger in the Labour Department. *The Palm-Wine Drinkard* might never have been written if Tutuola had not received this boon' (e-mail to author, 17 November 1998).

For all practical purposes, the story should end here, but it does not. In 1975, Lindfors discovered a reference to the forgotten manuscript in a letter from the Focal Press to Faber and Faber after the publication of *The Palm-Wine Drinkard*. Lindfors had been reading through Faber and Faber's file on the Nigerian writer and contacted the Focal Press. After several months, the manuscript of the unpublished novel was located. Faber and Faber (at Lindfors' prompting) then located the original handwritten manuscript of *The Palm-Wine Drinkard*. Together, according to Lindfors, the two manuscripts represented 'the genesis of contemporary Nigerian literature in English' ('Postscript' to *The Wild Hunter in the Bush of Ghosts*, p. 160).

Not surprisingly, *The Wild Hunter in the Bush of Ghosts* shares a number of features with *The Palm-Wine Drinkard*, as it does with all of Tutuola's published works. The narrator, the Wild Hunter, undertakes an arduous journey after the death of his father, wandering from village to village in the bush of ghosts and meeting a plethora of unusual characters (including illegitimate ghosts and cannibal ghosts) and unanticipated situations. Readers have been particularly struck by one section of the episodic narrative, set in the Devil's Town, which describes a bureaucracy so Kafkaesque that it is surprising that anyone ever manages to reach the world of the dead:

> The Exchange Manager, explained to us that if somebody would die in ten years to come, they would get their Records before then, and he told us again that only few people would be for God, but the rest would be for them in the hell. After the Exchange Manager had shown us all the Records, then we went to the Office of the Chief Secretary to the Hell, and we met him in his Office, then his clerk gave us chairs and we sat at his front. After a few minutes the Chief Secretary to the Hell accompanied us to his staff Office and there we met 2607 clerks, but they were very busy by the time we met them, and the works of this Chief Secretary to the Hell would be explained later. (p. 121)

This passage and others further illuminate Tutuola's remark about his stultifying position at the Department of Labour. Of equal interest, because of its autobiographical implications, is the fact that the Wild Hunter undertakes his journey *after* his father's death, suggesting that the Tapster in the novel published earlier is a surrogate father figure.

Lindfors knew that he had unearthed two major literary discoveries, particularly with the manuscript of the first novel which Tutuola himself had forgotten about. Briefly in London instead of at his usual location at the University of Texas, he wrote a hasty letter to Tutuola (whom he had met on several occasions and with whom he had had a sporadic correspondence), informing the writer of the discoveries. As would any serious scholar, Lindfors immediately became concerned about preserving the two manuscripts. In his letter to the author, he proposed that the manuscript of *The Palm-Wine Drinkard* be sold to the Humanities Research Center at Texas, but he emphasized that the Center would need to appraise the material before making any firm offer. Lindfors also assumed that Tutuola would want to sell the manuscript, though he indicated that he also hoped that Faber and Faber would want to publish *The Wild Hunter in the Bush of Ghosts* since it had never appeared in print (it was still the property of the Focal Press).

Lindfors then made two errors of judgement, the first being his proposal to take temporary possession of the manuscript of *The Palm-Wine Drinkard* in order 'to inspect it more closely'. In his letter to Tutuola of 24 March 1978, he explained:

> I am not a wealthy man but I could offer you 100 Naira for it immediately. My university, which has a Humanities Research Center that collects important twentieth century manuscripts, might be able to offer you more than that but they probably would not be able to pay you the full amount until next September, when they receive their budget for the 1978–79 academic year. I would be happy to try to arrange for them to buy it at the fairest possible price, if you are interested in the possibility of selling it to them. The manuscript would then remain in their library and would be made available to scholars, students and others who wanted to come to the library to read and study it, but all legal rights to the manuscript would remain in your hands or in the hands of your heirs. No one would be able to publish it, or portions of it, without your permission. This would certainly be the best arrangement for preserving the manuscript and safeguarding your own interests in it. If you decide you would prefer to sell the manuscript to me now for 100 Naira in immediate cash, I would be willing to try to negotiate a later resale of the manuscript to the Humanities Research Center ... In other words, I would not attempt to make any personal profit from resale of the manuscript. My concern would be to ensure that the manuscript is properly preserved and that you are adequately compensated for it, if you decide to sell it. (quoted in 'On Shocks, Sharks and Literary Archives', *Daily Times*, 15 July 1978)

Hereafter, the story takes on an ironic atmosphere of international intrigue. Communication with Tutuola was complicated; Lindfors' travel itinerary for the next few months was elaborate; there was a change in the senior position at the Humanities Research Center. Nevertheless, Tutuola responded (10 April) that he was delighted about the recent discoveries, adding in typical Tutuolan style, 'my sons and daughters are still wondering greatly how you could trace out this manuscript. They suggest that perhaps you were a police man before.' He then granted Lindfors permission to take temporary charge of the manuscript because he was interested in selling it to the Humanities Research Center. And, yes, he hoped that Faber and Faber would publish *The Wild Hunter in the Bush of Ghosts.*

Tutuola, however, soon changed his mind – or someone changed it for him. At the end of the month, Lindfors received a telegram attributed to the writer but actually written by Kole Omotoso (Lindfors, e-mail to author, 7 March 1999), that read as follows: 'PLEASE IGNORE MY APRIL 10 LETTER I HAVE CHANED MYMIND ABOUT MY MANUSCRIPT ANOTHER LETTER FOLLOWS' (errors in original). In the subsequent letter, Tutuola requested that the manuscript of *The Palm-Wine Drinkard* be returned to him 'because I like to see it once more ... after you have read it please send it back to Faber and Faber within two weeks. So soon as you have sent it to them, I shall write them to send it to me.' A month or so later, a friend informed Lindfors about an article by Yemi Ogunbiyi, published in the Nigerian *Daily Times* of 10 June 1978 and titled 'Tutuola in an Ocean of Sharks'.

This lengthy diatribe begins with an attack on Faber and Faber: 'Tutuola has, to put it mildly, been cheated by his publishers. He is the victim of what might well be the greatest swindle of a living African artist by a foreign publishing firm.' The language is inflammatory but the specifics are, indeed, disturbing: Tutuola's English publisher is accused of licensing the American edition and the foreign translations of *The Palm-Wine Drinkard* without paying a penny to the author. He continues: 'Tutuola is the victim of the combined circumstances of history and unvirtuously callous sharks who pass for publishers ... In 1978, we are still being offered glass-beads for our gold.' And then, in the most disturbing statement in the attack, Ogunbiyi claims: 'in the 21 years that [sic] Faber and Faber of London published *The Palm-Wine Drinkard*, Amos Tutuola was paid exactly £559.52 (about N951) in royalties,' though no explanation is offered for this accounting.

If these figures are correct, it would be difficult not to agree with Ogunbiyi's complaints. What did happen to the royalties from the American edition and the foreign translations of Tutuola's first published novel? Did the royalties from the British edition amount to only £559.52 in over twenty years? What about subsidiary rights for portions of the novel that were published in anthologies and/or textbooks, including several of my own anthologies for which my publishers paid Faber and Faber and Grove Press several hundred dollars? And what about the movie rights to the novel that were sold to Walt Disney?[3]

It is easy to understand why Ogunbiyi links Tutuola's fate as a writer to what he describes as:

> the unceasing exploitation of black artists, especially the musicians and performers, by the sharks of promoting companies. Lacking the much-needed economic base and strength to drive hard bargains, black artists in America are perpetually at the complete mercy of the few big promoting and publishing companies who, as they say in America, 'call all the shots' and dare to prescribe not just how they must write but fix what they, the publishers, will pay. Obviously, Tutuola faced this problem in 1951 and many of our writers, particularly, the aspiring ones, do face it today.

Ogunbiyi questions the issue of copyright, as well as raising several minor concerns, including why the original manuscript for *The Palm-Wine Drinkard* was never returned to Tutuola, before launching an attack on Professor Lindfors:

> But it is the despicable role of Lindfors that is even the more disturbing now, especially because it comes from an American, so-called liberal scholar who parades himself not only as an authority of some sort on our literature, but a good friend of many of our artists. His role confirms the point that many of our writers (Achebe, Soyinka, Armah of Ghana, Ngugi of Kenya) have said again and again and that is, that a majority of the Europe American adventurer-critic-friends of our literature are more shameless opportunists who exploit the fact that ours is a young literature still waiting to be most competently evaluated.

As for the manuscript, Ogunbiyi implies, how dare Lindfors suggest such a paltry sum 'for a manuscript which Lindfors himself knows is worth a fortune. And this offer comes from a man who knows very

---

3. See Harold R. Collins, *Amos Tutuola* (New York: Twayne, 1969), pp. 76–7.

well that Tutuola is today a penniless, exploited, retired and un-employed man.' I doubt that Lindfors had any accurate sense of Tutuola's economic plight; nor is there much evidence that Nigerians had been particularly concerned about his well-being until the dis-covery of the two early manuscripts. Yet Ogunbiyi cannot resist one final twist of the knife: 'Lindfors' position, implies, no matter how concealed, a cultural arrogance that smacks insipidly of presumptive condescension and even racism.'

The diatribe concludes on a happier note. Nigerian writers and critics – Kole Omotoso, Wole Soyinka, and Professor Aboyade, the vice-chancellor at Ife University – have 'initiated a move to retrieve the original manuscripts' and employ Tutuola 'as a Visiting Fellow' at Ife University. Tutuola, reportedly, will be paid N1000 by the uni-versity for the original manuscript of *The Palm-Wine Drinkard* – more than he is alleged to have received from twenty-one years of royalties. Furthermore, 'Tutuola has retained the legal services of the reputable Nigerian firm of Odujinrin, Adefulu, Ayanlaja and Co.,' to negotiate new contracts for his books with Faber and Faber and to 'serve as his literary agents'.

The Tutuola story was a *cause célèbre* in the Nigerian press for several weeks, with additional articles often skewing the initial in-formation. In an essay by Hassan M. Harding, headed 'Beyond Upholding Tutuola's Dignity' (*Daily Times*, 28 June 1978), the original figure for the accumulated royalties (£559.52) becomes N471, a much smaller figure. In 'Amos Tutuola – Victim of Exploitation' (*Sunday Times*, 2 July), Jide Osikomaiya states that Faber and Faber sent Tutuola additional money, presumably for the Grove Press edition and the translations of the novel. The amount, however, is not specified. Tutuola is quoted several times in this article, coming across, as he always did, as a gentle soul (a trait that some of his supporters claim made him particularly vulnerable to exploitation). Of the original acceptance of his novel, Tutuola states disarmingly: 'Honestly, I thought I should pay Faber and Faber for publishing my works. I didn't know they were capitalising on my talents. I never had the feeling that they were cheating me, after all nobody in Nigeria was ready to publish me even up to now.' The latter statement lays out quite clearly one of the major problems that Tutuola encountered virtually all of his life: where were the Nigerian publishers when he needed them? Tutuola adds: 'There was no other publisher around, especially in Africa. Faber and Faber took a risk with my work. They didn't expect it would bag a lot of money or get across to the reading masses.'

One cannot help reading these remarks without a certain amount of sadness. When Osikomaiya asks Tutuola if he believes that he has 'influenced Nigerian literature', the writer responds, 'I don't think so'. Osikomaiya had begun his article by stating: 'A lot of us Nigerians even after the recent newspaper publications would still wonder who Amos Tutuola is.' Even the opening paragraph of Yemi Ogunbiyi's exposé included the following remark: '[Tutuola] is the one-time store-keeper-turned writer whose rather limited knowledge of the grammar and rather tedious syntax of the English language became something of an advantage in his attempt to tell his many stories.' What one hand gives, the other takes away.

At the end of 1982, more than four years after the recovery of the two manuscripts, Three Continents Press in Washington, DC published Tutuola's *The Wild Hunter in the Bush of Ghosts*, 'Edited and with an Introduction and Postscript by Bernth Lindfors'. The volume includes a holograph reproduction of the original text and, on adjoining pages, a typed version for easier reading, complete with Tutuola's original emendations. The copyright is in Tutuola's name. The 'Introduction' and the 'Postscript' (with a tongue-in-cheek subtitle, 'Another Hunter's Tale') summarize the events that led to Lindfors' discovery of the manuscript, as well as the attack on his motives in the Nigerian press. More revealing, however, are the subsequent details of Tutuola's life and events leading up to the Three Continents' edition of the author's first narrative:

neither manuscript is in a Nigerian archive. Both are back in the hands of Amos Tutuola, but no university library or national institution has come forward with an offer to purchase them. Tutuola was employed for a year at Ife University, but the University has not yet followed up on its well-publicized intention to acquire his papers, and Ife University Press has not yet published any of his works. This is extremely disappointing, and perhaps Nigerians eloquent in expressing their concern for preserving national cultural treasures should begin to ask why nothing has happened. (p. 164)

After being skewered by the Nigerian press, Faber and Faber decided not to publish *The Wild Hunter in the Bush of Ghosts*. Kraszna-Krausz sold the original manuscript to Three Continents Press which, after publishing it in a limited edition, returned the manuscript to the author. Seemingly, the story of Tutuola's ongoing struggle to be a writer – to find an audience (both at home and abroad) and gain the respect of those readers with recognition that he was an important writer – would finally reach a stage of tranquillity. Tutuola could rest on his laurels, become the elder statesman of Nigerian writers, receive adequate renumeration for his efforts, and live a comfortable life. But the story does not achieve that stage of quiescence.

After his year of employment at Ife University, Tutuola was on his own again. The university never came through with the promised money for the original manuscript of *The Palm-Wine Drinkard*, if promise is what it was. Tutuola hoped that a buyer for the manuscript – possibly the federal government – would keep it in Nigeria. An American academic, Bob Wren, who was teaching at Ibadan University, helped the author prepare *Yoruba Folktales* for publication by Ibadan University Press (1986), editing Tutuola's colourful language into 'standard' English. Wren also suggested, as had Lindfors, that the Humanities Research Center consider the purchase of the original manuscript of *The Palm-Wine Drinkard*. The Center eventually paid $5000 for it and subsequently acquired additional materials from the author through an American agent. Thus, the Humanities Research Center at the University of Texas became the major repository for holdings of the Nigerian writer (Lindfors, e-mail to author, 17 November 1998).

One might assume that the accumulated royalties on Amos Tutuola's books would have supported him for the remainder of his life. Particularly during the 1970s and 1980s, black studies courses in the United States should have generated enough interest in his work to ensure a steady sale of *The Palm-Wine Drinkard*, the only title that has remained in print. During the last decade of Tutuola's life, however, sales in the United States fell off, averaging about 2000 copies per year (Nancy Flower, Grove Press, letter to author, 12 November 1998). In 1987 Faber and Faber published his final novel, *Pauper, Brawler and Slanderer*, and three years later a collection of his short stories, *The Village Witch Doctor and Other Stories*. A Yoruba edition of *The Palm-*

Wine Drinkard never appeared in Nigeria, although Tutuola himself completed the translation for a small publishing house. Assumptions about the cumulative sales of Tutuola's works are deceptive.

Correspondence with Bernth Lindfors has revealed that it was Lindfors himself who paid the $1000 Kraszna-Krausz wanted for the manuscript of *The Wild Hunter in the Bush of Ghosts* in order that Three Continents could publish it. The holograph edition of the book was published in a limited printing of 250 copies, but even a subsequent 'popular' edition of the book had only mediocre sales. The royalties on both editions were paid directly to Tutuola (Lindfors, e-mail to author, 17 November 1998).

Concerning the other royalties on his books (including the money from the American editions which pass through Faber and Faber), it is impossible to determine if Tutuola ever fully understood the accounting procedures. Lindfors, who in the 1970s read Faber and Faber's early correspondence with the author (including the royalty statements), concluded that Tutuola's English publisher was scrupulous in its treatment of him. Often, Tutuola would ask his editor to purchase something for him that he could not buy in Nigeria (such as a set of tyres for his car), ship it to him, and deduct the expenses from his royalty account. Moreover, Faber and Faber stuck by their author, publishing (after *The Palm-Wine Drinkard* and *My Life in the Bush of Ghosts*) six other books: *Simbi and the Satyr of the Dark Jungle* (1955), *Feather Woman of the Jungle* (1962), *Ayaiyi and His Inherited Poverty* (1967), *The Witch-Herbalist of the Remote Town* (1981), *Pauper, Brawler and Slanderer* (1987) and *The Village Witch Doctor and Other Stories* (1990). (Grove Press also published another of Tutuola's works, *The Brave African Huntress*, in 1958.)

Much of the correspondence between Tutuola and Faber and Faber has now disappeared, having been loaned by Tutuola to a Nigerian academic who never returned it. My own requests to Faber and Faber for an accounting of the author's royalties through the years have been denied. And what about the money that Tutuola should have received from Walt Disney for the movie rights to *The Palm-Wine Drinkard*? Attorneys at Disney have refused to answer my questions about the matter, though I have asked them repeatedly what happened to the property.

Amos Tutuola died on 7 June 1997, at the age of seventy-seven. A month and a half later, Bernth Lindfors received a request from Ayo Alegbeleye, Yinka Tutuola and Bunmi Tutuola (dated 25 July) that he contribute funds to be used for a proper burial for the writer. The missive included the following statement:

> A large member of the deceased's literary friends, colleagues and old students have indicated a strong desire to pay their last respect in terms of script-readings, stage-plays, dance-dramas, poetries etc at the burial. Even the Performing Artists are planning a star-parade. Expectedly, expenses are unavoidably high, despite efforts to cut down on activities. In this respect, we shall be very grateful for your financial assistance to offset some of these expenses. Any amount given shall be declared to the public through the press.

Yinka Tutuola, the writer's oldest son, included instructions as to where the money could be wired. Tutuola had died in poverty, leaving an extended family of four wives and eleven children. Lindfors made copies of this request and circulated the document widely in the United States, along with a cover letter explaining where money could be sent.

The Nigerian press rallied around the author, paying him lavish tributes and the kind of attention he rarely received during his lifetime. In 'A "Proper Farewell" to Amos Tutuola' (an overview of the response), Lindfors states that 'no fewer than five national dailies carried lengthy editorials summing up his career and achievements. To all of them he was a hero, a legend, a spellbinding raconteur, indeed, a storytelling genius', who won the respect of younger writers and journalists who referred to him as Pa Tutuola.

Nevertheless, his funeral was poorly attended and badly organized. Tunde Aremu, who observed the event, wrote in the *ALA Bulletin*: 'For so great a man, at least in the world of the literati, his burial would be expected to serve as a meeting point by not only the clan of writers, but of lovers of words, critics and other patrons of the arts. However, he went away as anonymous as he lived.' Though organized by the Association of Nigerian Authors with events intended to last two days (3 and 4 October), several organizers were not present.

If the first day was not indicative of the funeral of a man acknowledged to have made a mark in the literary world, the second day was abysmal. Said an arts writer who handles the book review page of a Lagos-based newspaper, 'I had thought many writers even from foreign nations will be here.' He had expected too much, we had all expected too much; the only public figure at the burial was Ambassador Olusegun Olusola. Other notable figures were Professor Dapo Adelugba of the Theatre Arts Department, University of Ibadan, Odia Ofeimun, and Dr. Bode Sowande. Apart from these, there were people mostly known in the literary world, and they were hardly up to ten.

Tutuola's family had asked the governments of Oyo and Ogun states for assistance for the funeral but did not even receive an acknowledgement of their request. According to Aremu, the only memorable moment was during Ordia Ofeimun's oration: '[Tutuola] had only a donkey for his journey; but it was his fate, his destiny to feed the donkey until it became a horse.'

Cyprian Ekwensi – one of Tutuola's Nigerian peers and another writer who has suffered many of the same indignities – stated at the time of the author's death: 'Tutuola wrote music with his words. Although his medium was prose, his writing appeared more musical, more lyrical and more poetic than many of those who actually set out to write poetry' (quoted in Lindfors, 'A "Proper Farewell"'). Ekwensi hoped that Nigeria would establish a national literary award in honour of his deceased friend, that proper recognition for the writer would finally emerge from home instead of abroad. He noted, however, 'Recognition in Nigeria today is based on how much money a man has ... People want to know the cars he owns, the clothes he wears. Nobody asks how people get money. Nobody bothers about excellence in anything.' One cannot help but detect the bitterness in Ekwensi's remarks. Indeed, years earlier, he had stated that his novels – several with multiple printings and international editions – had brought him both fame and poverty; a statement that is also true of Amos Tutuola's career.

Nor can one ignore the fact that, even at his death, too many Nigerians were not quite certain who Amos Tutuola was or what he had written. Few had read his books and, even among those who had, there was still the lingering feeling that all Tutuola had done was write down tales that everybody, or at least his fellow Yorubas, already knew. T. A. Oyesakin, of Lagos State University, reiterated what others had articulated on many earlier occasions:

> If you translate [Tutuola's] works to Yoruba language, a Yoruba man – who doesn't speak any other language – would simply assume that you are boring him with a story he listens to on a daily basis. By 15, a typical Yoruba child is conversant with the folktales. And in telling them, you bring in your own additive … [Amos Tutuola] follows the pattern of story telling, but he did not do so creatively. In other words, he did not put in the details which the African story teller would put in. He only makes do with the skeleton. (quoted in Lindfors, 'A "Proper Farewell"')

For Oyesakin – and for other Nigerians still uncomfortable with Tutuola's work almost fifty years after it was first published – Tutuola was little more than a scribe, writing down the obvious, the familiar, what was already known. He is still an embarrassment, someone who never should have had all that attention; the implication, as always, is that any Yoruba could have done what Tutuola did.

But the fact of the matter is, no one else did, which is part of the genius of every individual artist. There is only one *Things Fall Apart*, in spite of the fact that many Africans were familiar with accounts of the first Europeans invading their communities. There is only one *L'enfant noir (The Dark Child)*, in spite of the fact that other Franco-phone African students besides Camara Laye ended up in France, believing they would never return to their homelands. And there is only one *Palm-Wine Drinkard*, in spite of the Yoruba novels by Chief Fagunwa and numerous collectors of Yoruba folklore.

Late in life, when asked why he wrote, Amos Tutuola provided the best explanation for his craft and his artistry, defending himself as a preservationist of his own culture: 'I don't want the past to die. I don't want our culture to vanish. It's not good. We are losing [our customs and our traditions] but I'm still trying to bring them into memory' (Lindfors, 'A "Proper Farewell"'). For many readers of African literature, Amos Tutuola captured those memories, locking them unforgettably into the written word.

. . . .

CHAPTER 2

'Talking with Paper' is Only the Beginning

This is what this book on the politics of language in African literature has really been about: national, democratic and human liberation. The call for the rediscovery and the resumption of our language is a call for a regenerative reconnection with the millions of revolutionary tongues in Africa and the world over demanding liberation. It is a call for the rediscovery of the real language of humankind: the language of struggle. It is the universal language underlying all speech and words of our history. Struggle. Struggle makes history. Struggle makes us. In struggle is our history, our language and our being. That struggle begins wherever we are; in whatever we do: then we become part of those millions whom Martin Carver once saw sleeping not to dream but dreaming to change the world. (Ngugi wa Thiong'o, *Decolonising the Mind: The Politics of Language in African Literature*, 1986)

The real question is not whether Africans *could* write in English but whether they *ought to*. Is it right that a man should abandon his mother-tongue for someone else's? It looks like a dreadful betrayal and produces a guilty feeling.

But for me there is no other choice. I have been given this language and I intend to use it. I hope, though, that there will always be men, like the late Chief Fagunwa, who will choose to write in their native tongue and ensure that our ethnic literature will flourish side-by-side with the national ones. For those of us who opt for English there is much work ahead and much excitement …

I feel that the English language will be able to carry the weight of my African experience. But it will have to be a new English, still in full communion with its ancestral home but altered to suit its new African surroundings. (Chinua Achebe, *Morning Yet on Creation Day*, 1965)

§ IN the United States (and indeed in much of the western world), would-be writers submit their poems or short stories to magazines, journals and newspapers. It's an easy enough process, in part because there are plenty of publications around. If they stick with the process of submission, polish their craft, and develop thick skins, chances are that eventually someone will publish their work. The same applies, though with a more limited chance of acceptance, to a novel or other book-length manuscript. The pages of *Publishers Weekly* and the style sections of newspapers and magazines are bursting with accounts of writers who have hit the jackpot financially and become celebrities. True, this year's celebrity may be next year's dead horse, but stories of successful writing careers often take on a life of their own.

Few of these aspects of publishing apply to African writers. When Amos Tutuola finished writing his first two novels, he was not aware of any publishers in Nigeria who would be interested in his works. He sent his first manuscript to the Focal Press because he was familiar with their photography books; it probably never occurred to him that the Focal Press published only technical works. His second book, *The Palm-Wine Drinkard*, was sent to the United Society for Christian Literature because of an advertisement he had seen in *Nigeria Magazine* and, perhaps more importantly, because his education had been at mission schools.

Tutuola was fortunate in gaining Faber and Faber as a publisher. The delays were considerable, but the book was eventually published. In the years when Tutuola began writing, the post was reliable, even sacrosanct. That didn't mean, however, that there were never mishaps. In 1957, after completing *Things Fall Apart*, Chinua Achebe sent the handwritten manuscript of the only copy along with a postal order for £32 to a secretarial service in London for typing. The figure itself is worth noting; it was a large sum for an African to pay for such services at a time when the annual per-capita income in Nigeria was approximately £30.

Whether or not the typing agency was a legitimate one is difficult to determine, but after many months (and several query letters), the typed manuscript did not arrive. A friend who was travelling to London went to the agency to inquire about the status of the typing. According to Achebe's biographer, Ezenwa-Ohaeto, the manuscript was gathering dust in a corner of the office. After it was finally typed, Achebe had the rare services of a literary agent who eventually sold his novel to William Heinemann. Achebe told Alan Hill, his editor, that if the manuscript had been lost or stolen, 'I would have been so discouraged that I would probably have given up altogether. Even if I had forced myself to write the book again, it would have been a different book' (p. 63). One wonders how many manuscripts by African writers have been lost in the post or mislaid in publishing houses.

For most African writers today, submitting a manuscript is still a process fraught with difficulties. There are still too few publishers to fulfil the needs of the continent's writers. Literary journals, magazines, newspapers and other publications willing to print short stories and poems are few in number, even in densely populated countries such as Nigeria and South Africa. Even fewer of them pay their contributors. Although a number of significant publications have appeared in recent decades, many – including some with university backing – have had brief lives. And African writers have not been much more successful in submitting their stories and poems to European or American publications than they were in the 1950s. Once again, the delays are enormous, the post unreliable, and many writers have little accurate knowledge about which publications might be most receptive to their work.

With African publishing houses, as we will later see in more detail, the situation is not significantly better. Although there are, in fact, several hundred publishers in sub-Saharan Africa, most of them do not publish creative works, concentrating instead on technical works or non-fiction for the educational market. Those that publish fiction, poetry and drama, besides being few in number, are often unsupportive or incapable of nurturing creative writers, dishonest in their accounting methods, and marginal enough that many writers still look abroad, especially to the UK and France, for a publisher. Obviously, there are exceptions, but the number of publishing houses throughout Africa that have been supportive of the creative endeavours of black African writers can probably be numbered in single figures. Nevertheless, African writers have been attempting to address these issues for many years.

Onitsha Market Literature

In the early 1960s, when I taught English in a boys' secondary school not far from Onitsha in the eastern region of Nigeria, I encountered enormous difficulties in preparing my students for their School Certificate Examinations. These problems were not related to learning difficulties, because my students were the most industrious I have encountered in forty years of teaching; rather, the issues were cultural. In those days the material for examinations had not been Africanized, so all of the selections for literature were works by British writers. Victorian novels – I remember Thomas Hardy's *Far from the Madding Crowd* particularly – were daunting simply because of their length. A novel of several hundred pages was often overwhelming for students whose first language was Igbo. Yet with determination, even the length of the work was less intimidating than what the story contained: unfamiliar settings, characters who were radically unlike the people around them, situations that were perplexing if not downright incomprehensible. Why, for example, was there all this fuss about men and women getting together sexually? The western concept of romantic love was particularly difficult to comprehend, and western sexual practices were even more confusing. 'Excuse, sir,' one of my students said to me after class one day, 'what does it mean "to kiss"?'

At the time, I thought my student was indeed unworldly, but it was my own ignorance that was in operation here. I had no idea that kissing (and sexual foreplay) are not universal practices, driven by biological factors. No wonder all those flustered encounters between Gabriel Oak and Bathsheba Everdene were incomprehensible to my students, especially those kisses (or, more accurately, missed kisses). No wonder much of the literature they read made little sense.

Astute as they were, Nigerians – and Ibos specifically – had already begun writing their own stories (or 'talking with paper', to borrow a term from Wole Soyinka) that catered to Nigerian readers culturally, educationally and economically. Onitsha Market Literature began during the aftermath of the Second World War when literacy in English was higher than it had been at any previous point, money was available for something beyond the bare necessities, and printing presses were ready to begin producing indigenous material for an emerging literate class.

One of my secondary school students, J. ('Joseph') U. Tagbo Nzeako, presented me with a copy of his own novel, *Rose Darling in the Garden of Love*, printed for him at one of the Onitsha print-shops. Examining my copy more than thirty-five years later, I remember it as my introduction to a cultural phenomenon that was addressing itself to the real world and not to the academic discourse of the classroom.

Rose Darling in the Garden of Love has a text of twenty-nine pages, preceded by several introductory sections. Printed on newsprint which is now badly deteriorated, the cover is of slightly heavier material, once green but now considerably faded. Besides the title and the author's name, the cover identifies the writer as 'Formerly Of DR OKONGWU MEMORIAL GRAMMAR SCHOOL., NNEWI' (informing the potential purchaser that the author has reached the level of a secondary school education, no minor achievement in those days) and the printer/publisher as 'Tabansi Bookshop, 55 New Market Road, Onitsha'. The price is 1s. 6d. The cover graphics are limited to a simple border of interwoven flowers and vines. The title page repeats all of the information on the cover but omits the price. This is followed by a table of contents (providing the titles of the twelve chapters), an acknowledgements page, a Preface, and two 'Forewords'. The acknowledgements are mostly to the author's teachers and friends at his grammar school, followed by a signed note: 'All the towns, characters and schools in this story are imaginary, and do not refer to any individual or institution. The story itself is also imaginary, therefore has no connection with any existing character', followed by the author's name.

The Preface begins, 'People of this Century love without bound. They admire beauties, marry beauty and think less of character,' and then shortly continues with the author's message: 'People ought to choose their life partners as those with whom they will share their lives, and not for the fact that the girls are very beautiful; or that the men have senior positions and probably ride cars' (p. 2) The didactic warning concludes by foreshadowing what will be Rose's own fate: 'Here is a story of the most seductive sweet heart who was given a poor training by her old, toothless mother, a meretrix [sic], who at sixty five, was in love with a boy of twenty. This illicit training caused her numerous disappointments and finally concluded her doom' (p. 3). The passage is once again followed by the author's name, but this time includes his mailing address.

The first Foreword, by Sunny Okolo, includes a passage about Nzeako's importance as a writer – 'I have no doubt that he will be a great writer in the near future. Nevertheless if you read his more interesting stories in printing, you will conclude that Nigeria has got a "Bacon"' – and concludes, 'I shall not hesitate to say that this book deserves a place in any library, and it will be of good taste to able novelists' (p. 4). The second Foreword, by Tommy A. Asiegbu, continues to stress the exemplary aspects of Nzeako's writing: '"Rose Darling in the Garden of Love" is an attempt to moral education of youths and old people, who had tasted the fruit of bitterness and those who would like to experiment. To be candid, this is an attempt made by a student, and it will not fail to inspire many students of literature, while I recommend this booklet to every Tom, Dick and Harry' (p. 5). The second Foreword is dated 22 July 1961 – the only date in the entire book since there is no copyright – which makes it possible to speculate that J. U. Tagbo Nzeako wrote the book immediately after he finished his primary school education.

The opening of Chapter 1 ('Rose Won Ola's Love') reads as follows:

> In a tiny two-room cabin at Adori, a village in Okom division was an old toothless woman, a meretrix, who was so mad with love making that at sixty, she was in love with a young man whose age was that of her grandson. This woman had a daughter, whose name was Rose, a bastard, who when she grew up was notorious for love making.
>
> Rose was in love with a young man of slender build, whose name was Ola. When they first met at the Sports Stadium, Ola immediately impressed her with his personality, his hairy body and his extraordinary charm. When Ola was going home, he purposely took the Bright Street which of course was the girl's street. The girl was sitting on the corridor of their house eating some eggs. Ola had just bought a new 'Raleigh Moped' and he wanted to show off; when he saw her, he glanced at her with interest. He increased the speed, but unfortunately struck a log, and fell off. Rose rushed out and picked up his moped for him and fetched him water to wash his hands. Ola,

with his colourful language and soft tune, expressed his appreciation for her hospitable behaviour towards him. Rose gazed at him with that instinctive look peculiar to most women; after which there followed an introduction from both sides and they bid each other 'Good Bye'. (p. 13)

Skimming these opening paragraphs in the Tabansi Bookshop, what schoolboy could resist paying 1s. 6d. for a copy of the book? Rose, the astute reader has already concluded, will live as her mother has lived, sexually promiscuous.

The story moves quickly. The day after his moped accident, Ola writes Rose a lengthy letter confessing his love for her. He is so enthralled, he writes, that he dreams of her while he is awake. Rose kisses his letter as she reads it. Soon, the two of them are married. Equally fast is Ola's almost immediate physical and psychological decline, due to an unnamed illness: 'He drank water, but his urine which accommodated younger maggots, took the colour of well prepared Quaker Oats' (p. 13). If the book were contemporary, Ola's death would probably be the result of AIDS, the subject of which has recently begun to permeate the fiction of the continent. After Ola's death, poverty-stricken Rose decides to move to another town and start life over again.

Rose has a brief infatuation/romance with Mossy, a student, but he wises up and abandons her when he returns to school. So Rose marries Eddy, who is older than she, seemingly for security rather than love. Then, once again, lust becomes her guiding force. She abandons her child and husband for another younger man, who in turn abandons her after he learns of her unfaithfulness. At this point, Rose seemingly gives up on life (and the author gives up on his story), and poisons herself with a cup of DDD (DDT?). 'Beside her dead body were vultures and birds, who were either mourning for her death, or were waiting for their breakfast' (p. 28). In keeping with its moralistic tone, the story concludes:

Rose, whom scores and hundreds of different lovers danced in the ballroom of her hungry, romantic heart, died alone in complete desolation; no one to kiss her drying lips, none to embrace her for the last and the worst of it all, none to do her that last honour usual to the departing.

Her inevitable doom, on the other hand, was typical of Heaven's final punishment to those in the shoes of Rose Darling, as the deceiver must never go undeceived. (p. 29)

The heavy-handed moralizing is not so far removed from that found in any number of celebrated western classics: *Manon Lescaut*, *Thérèse Raquin*, *Sister Carrie*. The introductory paraphernalia (the author's Preface and the two Forewords) replicates the attempts at verisimilitude found in similar framings of early western novels. One thinks of *Moll Flanders*, for example, or *Les liaisons dangereuses*, and the authors' claims that young readers, especially, will not be led astray by reading these books, which can serve as exemplary material. Such statements, of course, masked the salacious content of early western novels and were designed to sell books rather than to check immorality.

At first glance, J. U. Tagbo Nzeako's *Rose Darling in the Garden of Love* may seem unworthy of such lengthy analysis, insignificant in the emergent literature of a nation and a continent. Yet dozens of similar 'novels' flowed from the pens of the Onitsha writers, and, somewhat later, from their peers in other countries (Ghana, Kenya, South Africa, Zimbabwe) across the continent. The significance of this writing is that it provided a much-needed platform for 'new' writers, whose own literacy was not much beyond that of their readers.

The Onitsha pamphleteers (as they have often been called) wrote books that were inexpensively produced and therefore readily acquired, usually for a fraction of the cost of an imported book. Unlike imported texts, their stories were set in their readers' own environment, the situations were recognizable, as were the places and the characters. Again, the similarities between this literature and the origins of the novel in Europe, particularly in England and France, cannot be overemphasized. As is also true of early publishing in the West, the majority of the Onitsha publications were not works of fiction but chap-books, self-help books.

Self-help books have traditionally catered to the upstart, the person who wants to improve his (or her) lot in life. For centuries, etiquette books have appealed to those who want to rise in society but are afraid of making embarrassing social blunders. With the advent of Onitsha writing, suddenly there were books informing readers how to improve their own situations. Hence, titles such as *Quotations for All Occasions Wise Sayings, Idioms, Proverbs, Good English and Compositions* by Chidi M. Ohaejesi, who identifies himself as 'Freelance Journalist & Nig. Author'; or, *How to Organise Meetings and Know the Work of a Chairman, Secretary, Treasurer, Auditor, Financial-Secretary, Publicity Secretary, Provost, Committees Etc.* by Wilfred Onwuka, 'Author, Poet, Actor, Novelist and Dramatist'; or – my all-time favourite because of the typographical errors in the title, *How to Avoid Misatkes and Live a Good Life A Moral Instructions on Don'ts in Public Meetings, Social Gatherings and Functions for Boys & Girls, Workers and Traders* by K. C. Ezeh. Frequently, the self-help was fused with the personal (the search for a mate), as in such titles as *How to Make Friends with Girls* by J. Abiakam; *How to Speak to Girls and Win Their Love* also by J. Abiakam; *Beware of Harlots and Many Friends the World is Hard* by J. O. Nnadozie; and *How to Marry a Good Girl and Live in Peace with Her* (Anonymous). A much later variation of this topic is *The Nigerian Bachelor's Guide* by A. O. Ude, with question and answer responses such as the following (in the chapter 'Questions for Girls'): 'If your husband wants to flog you or has actually flogged you what will be your reaction? I shall do all I can to resist the flogging but I shall never fight him' (p. 49).

Political and topical issues were also compelling subjects for the Onitsha writers: *The Complete Trial of Adolf Hitler* by J. C. Anorue; *How Lumumba Suffered in Life and Died in Katanga* by Okenwa Olisa; and *The Life Story and Death of John Kennedy* by Wilfred Onwuka ('Master of Pen'). Fact and fiction merge in these topical booklets, often published in a matter of weeks after an historical event (such as Kennedy's assassination). In the latter title, which is narrated partly in dramatic form, President Kennedy (immediately after being shot) stands up in the vehicle in which he has been riding and delivers a lengthy speech, concluding:

> God have mercy on my soul and that of my killer, because he knows not what he did.
> Blessed be the land of America.
> Blessed be the people and rulers of the world.
> Blessed be the soul of Abraham Lincoln who died because of slavery and slave trade abolition in 1864.

Blessed be my dear father and mother.

Blessed be my brothers and sisters.

Blessed be my wife and children

Blessed be the American Negroes whom I am sacrificing my blood
for their own safety.

Blessed be my soul and good bye to my friends. (pp. 22–3)

Other early narrative accounts bear striking similarities to their western equivalents, such as *The Life in the Prison Yard – 'It Is a Hard Life'* by Okenwa Olisah, and the popular English narrative, *The Black Dogg of Newgate*, published in 1600.

Still, the most popular Onitsha titles were novels, thinly disguised sexual narratives typically between thirty and seventy pages in length, such as the ever-popular *Rosemary and the Taxi Driver* by Miller O. Albert; and *The Sorrows of Love* and *Agnes in the Game of Love*, both by Thomas Iguh. These bestsellers were sometimes reprinted so frequently that total sales reached 100,000 copies or even more. Additionally, most Onitsha publications – and this is certainly true of the literature for the masses from much of the continent – were shared among many readers. Like newspapers and other periodicals, they were passed from person to person until they fell apart.

One such ever-popular title is *Mabel the Sweet Honey that Poured Away* by Speedy Eric (A. Onwudiwe). A photograph on the cover shows a curvaceous Caucasian female in a low-cut dress and the following teaser: 'Her skin would make your blood flow in the wrong direction. She was so sweet and sexy, knew how to romance. She married at sixteen. But she wanted more fun. Yet it ended at seventeen. And what an – end? **So thrilling**.' Besides the resemblance that Mabel shares with any number of fallen heroines in western novels, *Mabel the Sweet Honey* is also close to western softcore pornography of a certain vintage. 'The highly aroused girl entivined her arms on his neck sucking back his lips too. At the same time Gil had his fingers in her hair ruffling the thing passionately' (p. 47). The text – so typical of many Onitsha pamphlets – is replete with typographical errors made by compositors who were barely literate themselves. But the high moral tone eventually trumps the salacious passages; Mabel dies a gruesome death after taking an 'overdose' (p. 69) of contraceptives. Could any reader fail to be engrossed?

In an article in *Transition* (published at the time in East Africa), Donatus I. Nwoga, an Ibo, estimated that by 1963 at least two hundred different Onitsha pamphlets had been published. My own estimate is that an additional hundred titles had appeared by 1967, when the Biafran war began. The Nigerian civil war virtually destroyed the Onitsha market, which had been perceived as a symbol of Ibo financial dominance in the country. Still, not long after the war was over, presses were again rolling, publishing accounts of what had happened during the struggle itself. The most scholarly study of this literature, *An African Popular Literature: A Study of Onitsha Market Pamphlets* by Emmanuel Obiechina, was published by Cambridge University Press in 1973. It includes not only an extensive analysis of the literature itself (with insights about romantic relationships; religion and morals; the influences of the cinema, the newspaper and Shakespearean language, as well as the romances of Marie Corelli and Bertha Clay on the writers) but also an exhaustive bibliography. About the curious romantic relationships depicted in Onitsha novels, Obiechina, for example, concludes:

> Romantic love, transplanted from its native Western soil onto the seemingly hostile and antipathetic soil of traditional Africa, has had such rich nourishment from an array of most disparate and incongruent nutrients that it has managed to survive in spite of the obvious odds. It has become one of the living realities of modern Africa and must therefore be taken into account by anyone who wishes to consider life on the continent and see it whole. Its existence has not been lost sight of by commentators on the state of society, least of all by the popular writers and artists who reflect the major, surface movements and appearances of the given moment. The writers of the Onitsha Market pamphlets are no exception. (p. 41)

Audience

It is difficult to read a work such as *Rose Darling in the Garden of Love* or *Mabel the Sweet Honey* and not be amused by the ludicrous situations, the hilarious dialogue and the typographical errors. A passage taken at random from *Mabel* reads as follows:

> One cheerful man who came in by eleven a.m. smacked Mabel on the

buttocks and exclaimed; 'Hah! If them give me this one I no go ask for more food any more' Mabel glared at the man who must not be less than thirty years. He had a squarish face but his arms were full of muscles. He was dark black but his skin was shining and clean as if it had been polished.

'Please, don't do that,' Mabel said seriously 'Okay juice, the man replied, 'but you are so much like honey that a man with a healthy appetite cannot help but try to dig his finger into it and lick and lick.'
(p. 35)

Similar amusement is inspired by western literature, when we consider equivalent examples. I have observed hysterical amusement among a class of undergraduates when I read them passages from American 'Dime Novels' written at the turn of the twentieth century. They responded in the same way to passages from Horatio Alger Jr novels, which in many ways are similar to Onitsha narratives. Time and culture become the stumbling blocks, leading to all kinds of preconceived notions about the contents of the works themselves. And cultural naïvety has always contributed to the acceptance or rejection of African literary works by western editors. There is the example, perhaps apocryphal, that many African scholars have cited for years. An African novelist is said to have had his work rejected because (as the cover letter stated), it was 'Not African enough'. Such an attitude by European editors, real or imaginary, must have a negative influence on the writer trying to determine his (or her) audience. For whom does the African writer write?

By the mere act of writing and publishing in Nigeria, the Onitsha writers made a bold statement about their audience: they were writing for African readers. This was only partly true of earlier writers, whose work began to appear after the Second World War, though Amos Tutuola will always be in a league by himself. He wrote, it seems to me, for his own people, but if European and American readers were more taken by his stories, well, that was fine but he wasn't going to bend in any way for them. Chinua Achebe's *Things Fall Apart* is a different matter, as can be illustrated by any number of passages within the text itself. For example, in Chapter 1: 'Okoye said the next half a dozen sentences in proverbs. Among the Ibo the art of conversation is regarded very highly, and proverbs are the palm-oil with which words are eaten' (p. 7). The anthropological explanation about the importance of proverbs (of orality) is unnecessary for Ibo readers and no doubt for most Africans, but Achebe must have anticipated a certain amount of confusion among western readers. Hence, the frequently unobtrusive or parenthetical explanations that Achebe uses throughout his novel, such as: 'He had a bad *chi* or personal god' (p. 18).

By sending the manuscript of *Things Fall Apart* to an English literary agent (who would presumably place the work with a British publisher), Achebe clearly took into consideration his western readers who would need assistance with culturally specific materials. But Achebe has also provided another explanation, which is that his own culture was changing so rapidly after the Second World War that much of the background material for his story (and others that would follow) was included in order that his own people would have a record of life as it once was, before it disappeared and was forgotten. As he wrote in a celebrated essay called 'The Writer as Teacher':

> The [African] writer cannot expect to be excused from the task of re-education and regeneration that must be done ... I for one would not wish to be excused. I would be quite satisfied if my novels (especially the ones I set in the past) did no more than teach my readers that their past – with all its imperfections – was not one long night of savagery from which the first Europeans acting on God's behalf delivered them. Perhaps what I write is applied art as distinct from pure. But who cares? Art is important but so is education of the kind I have in mind. (*Morning Yet on Creation Day*, p. 45)

Endless debates about the 'faithfulness' and 'authenticity' of certain African writers have provided lively discussion at academic conferences and in scholarly articles. Such disputes are in no way unique to writers from the African continent but, rather, are part and parcel of academic rancor in the troubled era of deconstruction, including controversy concerning the definition of a text. The Native American writer Hyemeyohsts Storm, author of the magnificent novel *Seven Arrows* (1972), for example, has repeatedly had his 'Indianness' questioned, in spite of being listed on the Cheyenne rolls and having been trained by numerous tribal elders.

So the on-going discussion of audience – for whom does an African writer write? – will continue to plague the discourse in the future just as it has in the past. Were the *négritude* poets (studying in France in the 1930s) addressing their works to their compatriots back home on the continent and in the West Indies, or to Europeans, hoping that their rhetoric would hasten the process of independence? Did black South African writers during the wretchedness of apartheid intend that their poems, stories, and novels would soothe the wounds of the oppressed or garner the respect or even the anger of their oppressors? Is it even possible to write for two contradictory audiences? Were the many passages that deal with human excrement and bodily functions in Ayi Kwei Armah's *The Beautyful Ones Are Not Yet Born* (1968) intended to shock the western reader or simply describe the reality of life in a society that was unable to implement a level of sanitation equal to that of the West? Are Wole Soyinka's poems and plays so esoteric that the average Nigerian cannot understand them? What did Yambo Ouologuem intend by the passage in *Le devoir de violence* (*Bound to Violence*, 1968) that describes a prostitute haemorrhaging because a dissatisfied customer has secreted a razor blade in a bar of soap which she uses to wash her vagina? By even mentioning a writer's 'intent', I am aware that I am treading on thin ice as far as academic critics are concerned, but most other readers do not even consider such matters when they come across that razor blade in the bar of soap. Most writers, no matter where they are, write because they want to be read, and most, I would argue, do not care too much who their readers are.

Fortunately, the question of audience is quite different today. Since the 1970s, literacy levels across the continent have greatly increased. In many countries an audience exists, willing and anxious to read African writers. The publishers of *Things Fall Apart* can now boast that the novel has sold several million copies on the continent itself (and several million more in the rest of the world). Achebe's master-piece can be read not only in the English-speaking African countries but, in translation, in the Francophone areas as well. Which brings us to the question of language itself.

Language

There is a crying need for African literature written in the in-digenous languages, in virtually every country across the continent.

Attempts to address this need have been limited almost exclusively to texts for the school market, particularly the primary schools where education traditionally has not been in the European languages but in the indigenous ones. Thus, governments and ministries of education have supported and even commissioned the writing of texts and creative works (stories, poems, and so on), aimed at the lower grades, but since education after primary school has in most countries been in English, French or Portuguese, literary works for those markets are typically in the 'imported' languages. Consequently, in many countries it has been difficult for readers to find adult material in the African languages.

Forty years after independence, many of the obstacles facing the growth of indigenous literature are the same as they have always been. If educational systems rely on imported textbooks, then those books will be written in European languages because western publishing houses simply do not have editors and production people capable of producing an African text. The orthographies for some African languages are fairly recent, contributing to a dearth of actual writers and readers. A number of African publishers attempting to produce indigenous texts have discovered that readers (and buyers) of books are not always interested. Production is often shoddy and makeshift, resulting in books that are unattractive and thus unable to compete with materials produced in the West.

Of more centrality to our analysis here, however, is the misconception – expressed by a number of writers and critics for nearly fifty years – that an African text, an African literary work, can be African only if it is written in an African language. Thus, the argument goes, *The Palm-Wine Drinkard* is not genuine African literature because it was written in English, but the novels by Chief Fagunwa, written about the same culture and in Yoruba, are 'authentically African'. Sometimes the argument has gone so far as to state that since the novel is an imported literary form (there were no novels in traditional Africa), even the concept of an African novel is a bogus one. Carried to its logical extreme, the purists would conclude that the only authentic African literature is folklore, the oral tradition.

Fortunately, some of these arguments have been rendered moot by the high visibility of several writers (Wole Soyinka, Ben Okri, Nuruddin Farah) who have won major literary awards in the West, as well as numerous other writers from the Global South who for the past two decades have achieved high visibility in the West (Salman Rushdie, Gabriel Garcia Marquez, Vikram Seth, to mention only three). Furthermore, if those who argue that the only genuine African literature is traditional, pre-dating written works, then doesn't the same argument need to be made of Western literature? Will the purists soon be arguing that anything after Old English is not an authentic literary work?

The only genuine issue, it seems to me, is the one of language: European vs African. This dispute, in fact, has been going on for years between Chinua Achebe and the Kenyan writer Ngugi wa Thiong'o. Others, of course, have entered into the discussion, but Achebe and Ngugi have been at its heart.

Mid-way through his literary career, Ngugi wa Thiong'o, having published five novels in English and in the process becoming the most widely read and respected East African writer, began writing in Gikuyu, his first language. His rationale was certainly genuine enough. Too many of his own people could not read English; consequently, the works he had published were unavailable to them. His thinking had also been filtered through a Marxist perspective and was further layered with strong feelings about what neo-colonialism had brought his people. In *Decolonising the Mind: The Politics of Language in African Literature* (1986) Ngugi wrote:

> The real aim of colonialism was to control the people's wealth: what they produced, how they produced it, and how it was distributed; to control, in other words, the entire realm of the language of real life … Take language as communication. Imposing a foreign language, and suppressing the native languages as spoken and written, were already breaking the harmony previously existing between the African child and the three aspects of language. Since the new language as a means of communication was a product of and was reflecting the 'real language of life' elsewhere, it could never as spoken or written properly reflect or imitate the real life of that community. This may in part explain why technology always appears to us as slightly external, *their* product and not *ours*. (p. 16)

Ngugi wanted to be understood by the masses; he began writing plays in Gikuyu, because they could be presented to illiterate audiences no matter where they resided in the country:

> I believe that my writing in Gikuyu language, a Kenyan language, an African language, is part and parcel of the anti-imperialist struggles of Kenyan and African peoples. In schools and universities our Kenyan languages – that is the languages of the many nationalities which make up Kenya – were associated with negative qualities of backwardness, underdevelopment, humiliation and punishment. We who went through that school system were meant to graduate with a hatred of the people and the culture and the values of the language of our daily humiliation and punishment. I do not want to see Kenyan children growing up in the imperialist-imposed tradition of contempt for the tools of communication developed by their communities and their history. I want them to transcend colonial alienation. (p. 28)

A similar desire to reach a broad popular audience instead of limiting his work to readers fluent in French led the Senegalese novelist Ousmane Sembene, in 1966, to shift from writing novels and short stories in French to working in the cinema. In the process of moving from one medium to the other, Sembene became one of his continent's foremost film-makers with a popular following, perhaps because many of his films were made in Wolof. How can these decisions to reach much wider audiences be denigrated – especially when their goal is to embrace people who are illiterate?

Ngugi, however, was unhappy that the shift he had made from a European to an African language was not emulated by other writers, especially those with the same visibility and prestige that he had achieved. He has written eloquently on the subject but also relentlessly, constantly criticizing others who continue to pursue their careers in English and French:

> In other words writers in African languages should reconnect themselves to the revolutionary traditions of an organised peasantry and working class in Africa in their struggle to defeat imperialism and create a higher system of democracy and socialism in alliance with all the other peoples of the world … it is precisely when writers open out African languages to the real links in the struggles of peasants and workers that they will meet their biggest challenge … It is then

that writing in African languages becomes a subversive or treasonable offence with such a writer facing possibilities of prison, exile or even death. (pp. 29–30)

After many years, Chinua Achebe has reduced his responses to a brief statement: anyone is free to write in any language he wants. By refusing to impose his perspective on others, Achebe has also won the argument. He made his position clear years ago: 'I feel that the English language will be able to carry the weight of my African experience. But it will have to be a new English, still in full communion with its ancestral home but altered to suit new African surroundings' (*Morning Yet on Creation Day*, p. 62).

If we go back once again to the years before the publication of *Things Fall Apart* (1958), it is easy to understand Achebe's decision to write in English. If he had written his novel in Igbo, where would it have been published? Certainly not in England. The Onitsha writers, essentially, wrote pamphlets a fraction of the length of *Things Fall Apart*. There is no evidence that Onitsha printers had the facilities to publish a book of two hundred pages; their readers wanted short, inexpensive, works with a fairly restricted vocabulary. Achebe's decision to employ English was obviously a pragmatic one. More Ibos (that is, his own people) could read English than Igbo at the time, since the Igbo orthography had only recently been developed. If he had written his novel in Igbo, his readers would not only have been limited to a fraction of his own people but, worse, would have been locked within his own ethnic group. There are approximately 250 languages and dialects in Nigeria, and few people in those other groupings would have been able to read an Igbo version of *Things Fall Apart*. Even more limiting, such a publication would never have been able to reach readers across the continent, which embraces another 750 languages and dialects. Or outside Africa.

As well as anyone, Achebe is familiar with the excesses of tribalism. African writing in European languages may be regarded by some intellectuals as unAfrican, contrary to indigenous values and traditions, but the legacy of colonialism cannot be obliterated by a reversion to African languages. Writing in European languages may, in fact, help break down tribal barriers. Furthermore, the language a writer employs is not the determining factor in his or her national identity.

Samuel Beckett wrote in French but was no less Irish for doing so. Vladimir Nabokov wrote many of his late novels in English (American English, no less) but was no less Russian for doing so. Returning to *Things Fall Apart*, wouldn't Achebe have seen that a translation of his novel into Igbo was undertaken if he thought there was justification for it? The choice of language is one of expediency, or pragmatism, but above all it reflects the writer's desire to reach the largest possible audience.

Economics

Issues of language and audience, while major determinants in the ultimate success of African writers, are not nearly as influential as economics. The bottom line is brutal: books are expensive in Africa. They always have been. It doesn't matter whether this is today, when a copy of *Things Fall Apart* sells for N175 ($1.75) in Nigeria, or in 1962, when Achebe's novel became the first title issued in Heinemann's African Writers Series and sold for 5s. 5d. Books are expensive, almost in the domain of luxury items, and therefore out of the reach of many Africans, including the middle class and in those educational contexts (primary and secondary schools and universities) where literary works find their natural audience. Today, too many Africans must spend their money on basic necessities: food, clothing, medicine, even pure drinking water.

Both imported titles and locally produced works are too expensive for many potential African readers. Comparative pricing is the best way to demonstrate this. In 1996, when *Things Fall Apart* sold for $5.99 in the American Anchor paperback, readers in Zimbabwe had to pay the equivalent of two additional American dollars for the same title in an imported Heinemann edition. Few Americans would be inconvenienced by paying six dollars for a copy of the novel, but eight dollars for a Zimbabwean, whose family income for the year is often no more than several hundred American dollars, is beyond the realm of the possible. In the summer of 1998 I visited Africa University in Mutare in Zimbabwe and spoke to members of the English faculty. They lamented the cost of books and confessed that students could not afford to purchase assigned titles for their classes. The library did not have sufficient copies for everyone to read. Faculty members were reduced to teaching 'extracts' from novels and book-length texts because, with limited copying facilities, that was the most that could be managed. This example can be replicated across the continent, and it applies to what westerners consider moderately priced books. Expensive textbooks in the technical fields may cost the equivalent of a sixth of a family's yearly income. What can the future of African education be with books priced as prohibitively as this?

Locally produced books may in some cases be less expensive than imported titles, but often not that significantly. Paper is expensive in most African countries and, unfortunately, is produced in only a few. Too many countries have to import the paper needed for book production, and African governments (not necessarily thinking about the consequences) often tax paper, thus further increasing the cost of a book. Furthermore, too many books printed in Africa are so poorly produced (often on the equivalent of newsprint) that they quickly deteriorate. At least an imported textbook or novel printed on better paper can be shared by many readers and will probably hold up, even in the tropics, for many years. To be sure, textbooks and educational materials produced for the primary school market are less expensive for students to purchase, but the quality is again often sub-standard.

A brief comment about African libraries is germane here. If books are expensive for individuals, they are no less so for libraries (both public libraries and those connected to educational institutions). Education systems in too many African countries are equally strapped for cash. Typically, money for books for libraries is available only after other expenses (salaries, classroom instruction) have been paid. Libraries as we think of them in the West do not exist in many African countries. In the most recent *UNESCO Statistical Handbook* (1998), the number of books held in the twelve public libraries in Benin are listed as totalling 37,000 volumes; in the twenty-six public libraries in Senegal, the total is 17,000 volumes; in Uganda the one library, which has seventeen service points, has 82,000 volumes; in Kenya, the public library with twenty-one service points has 603,000 volumes.

These figures are all the more revealing when the statistics for countries outside Africa are provided for comparison. Thus, the 3672 public libraries in Canada have a total of 70,077,000 volumes; the 1171 public libraries in Turkey hold 11,170,000 volumes; the 249 public libraries in Denmark (with a total number of 950 service points) hold 31,580,000 volumes. Estimates by the African Skies Library Foundation are that the United States (with a population considerably less than that of the African continent south of the Sahara) has forty times the number of libraries, and that figure does not even reflect the wider gap when actual book totals are compared. Worse, some countries in Africa have no national library; and the number of volumes in libraries connected to educational institutions borders on the non-existent. Tijan M. Sallah told me that there are no public libraries in his country, the Gambia, and the National Library has no computers or fax machines (interview, 17 June 1999). It is true to say that most Africans – with the exception of those living in major cities – have never set foot in a library. The mere idea of a library is foreign to them. When I interviewed Irene Staunton, the publisher of the Baobab Press in Harare, Zimbabwe (4 August 1998), and asked her what single change would leave the biggest mark on Baobab's bottom line, she responded, 'Library sales'.

For the African writer, such economic realities are inescapable. There are hundreds, perhaps even thousands, of writers across the continent. The success stories that we hear about writers in the West rarely apply to African writers. Yes, *Things Fall Apart* has sold eight million copies since it was first published and, most encouraging of all, more of those copies have been sold on the African continent than away from it. Achebe is certainly a household name. The same applies, no doubt, to Ngugi, whose first novel, *Weep Not, Child* (1964), has sold well over a million copies. But what other title or author even approaches these figures? Writing in 1988, Alan Hill – the revered Heinemann editor who discovered Achebe and later began the African Writers Series – stated that Achebe and Ngugi dominated the series: 'As recently as 1984, of the total sales revenue from the 280 AWS titles, almost one-third was contributed by Achebe's six books' (*In Pursuit of Publishing*, p. 144).

It should come as no surprise that there may be a handful of African writers, at most, who are able to support themselves by their writing alone. Most are also academics or government bureaucrats, or ex-writers who no longer consider themselves writers but something else. African writers cannot live on their royalties because there are too few periodicals (magazines or newspapers) willing to pay them for their efforts. Relying on western publications is problematic and no more than an occasional source of revenue for a few of them. Relying on royalties from locally produced books is too often an exercise in futility. Royalties from abroad – even for the most successful writers – are more deceptive than actual, as the following examples will demonstrate.

Correspondence with Grove Press – the American publisher of *The Palm-Wine Drinkard* – has revealed that recent American sales of that novel have been running at about two thousand copies a year, mostly (it is assumed) for the college market. The book is listed at $12.95 in its current edition. Thus, 2000 copies at $12.95 results in a gross of $25,900, a significant amount of money. Assuming a royalty of 10 per cent, the author's share becomes $2590, but this is only the figure to begin with. It is unclear whether George Braziller, the holder of the American copyright, gets a percentage of this royalty, but let's assume for the sake of argument that he does not, that it all goes to Tutuola's heirs. Thus the $2590 is sent to Faber and Faber in London, which takes its 50 per cent cut (standard in the trade) for licensing the American edition, thereby reducing the amount due to the author (or his heirs) to $1295, still perhaps a significant amount for someone living in a shattered economy. But American taxes must be taken from the author's portion, since Nigeria and the United States have no reciprocal agreement involving taxes. The American government takes a standard 30 per cent, or $388.50, thus reducing the portion for the author's estate to $906.50, before Nigerian taxes. (There are no taxes removed by the British government, since a reciprocal arrangement does exist between the UK and its former colonies.)

It is possible that Amos Tutuola's estate may actually receive a higher percentage of the American royalties than Chinua Achebe receives for the American edition of *Things Fall Apart*. I stress, however, that these figures are speculative, since I am not privy to publishing arrangements and have therefore made these projections from what are considered standard publishing terms. If Achebe's novel were to sell 50,000 copies per year in the United States – a not impossible figure since it is the most widely adopted African text in classrooms – the figures would look like this. The current Anchor edition at $8.95 results in a gross sales figure of $447,500, and the author's 10 per cent royalty becomes $44,750, which sounds like an enormous amount of money. But Achebe's current publisher has had to license its edition from Ivan Obolensky, who, as the original American hardback publisher, takes 50 per cent. Achebe's portion is reduced to $22,375, still a significant amount of money until we factor in Heinemann's 50 per cent for holding the original English contract. That reduces the author's portion to $11,187.50. Achebe's agent, who originally sold the book for him, takes his 10 per cent cut, or $1118.75, reducing the author's portion to $10,068.75. Then American taxes remove 30 per cent, or $3020.62, leaving $7,048.13 for the author *before* Nigerian taxes. Again, there are certain assumptions I have made in these calculations which may not be applicable (both examples are based on trade editions, with royalties based on the gross rather than the net). Achebe's contract with William Heinemann may have been renegotiated after the book became so successful, or Achebe, who currently lives and teaches in the United States, may not have to pay Nigerian taxes on his royalties. Still, African writers, and Third World writers in general, typically receive only a small portion of standard royalties when their books are published in the United States and Europe. When books are published for the educational market (rather than in trade editions), the royalty percentage may be no more than 5 or 7.5 per cent, calculated from the wholesale rather than the retail price of the book.

Years ago, Stanlake Samkange told me of his humiliation when examining his first royalty statement for *On Trial for My Country* (1966) and discovering that copies of his novel sold 'overseas' received reduced royalties. What did that mean? Since his publisher (Heinemann) was in England, all copies sold outside the United Kingdom – including in Samkange's Rhodesia (now Zimbabwe) – received the lesser royalty, presumably to offset more expensive distribution costs. Ergo, all African writers who publish outside the continent receive reduced royalties for copies of their books sold in their own countries. Samkange had never paid any attention to that clause in his contract until he had the brutal economic facts in his hands.

Appropriation and Other Impediments

The first time I met Chinua Achebe was in December 1972. Although I had lived only a short distance from him when I taught in Nigeria a decade earlier, our paths had never crossed. But after the

Nigerian civil war (which ended in 1970), during one of his many visits to the United States, we met in Washington, DC, where I teach. For our meeting, I took along a stack of books for him to autograph and in the process handed him a first edition of his third novel, *Arrow of God* (1964). Achebe examined the book carefully and then said something to the effect that he no longer owned a first edition of the book. When I asked why, he told me that during the civil war the Federalists had gone out of their way to bomb his house – located outside the main arena of the war. I couldn't fathom the idea of a government bombing the house of a writer simply because he had been on the other side. Are writers that important? In times of peace and harmony, they are completely ignored.

Achebe's remark has haunted me for years. If I'd been worthy of the occasion, I would have insisted that he keep the book, which he certainly had more right to than I did. A writer ought to have a complete set of the first editions of his books. Was my failure to give him the book due to my inability to understand the way that I had 'appropriated' African literature? Is appropriation even the correct term to describe what I had been doing: writing about African writers and promoting their works to American publishers? Can literature be appropriated in the same way that natural resources can be mined or taken from the earth? Is a western critic of non-western literature just another imperialist, stripping a country of its basic resources? By reviewing an African book or by writing a critical analysis of such a work, has a critic or scholar from one culture appropriated something from another? If an African literary critic reviewed the latest novel by, say, American novelist Anne Tyler and spent his (or her) entire career writing about Tyler's oeuvre, would that also be considered appropriation?

I ask these questions because they are related to the dilemma that African writers face in having to publish overseas: they are therefore forced to rely on critical judgements made by people outside their cultures who may not understand what they have written ('not African enough'). It is bad enough that non-African editors in European and American publishing houses make the decisions about what to publish from Africa (or elsewhere in the non-western world). It becomes a double blow that these books are reviewed by western critics after they are published. If they were not reviewed and further analysed by

western critics – if a hands-off policy prevailed so the only commentary would come from Africa – what would be the success of
these books?

In an essay called 'Colonialist Criticism' in *Morning Yet on Creation
Day* (1975), Achebe had this to say about my analysis of Ayi Kwei
Armah's writing: 'An American critic, Charles Larson, makes good
use of this kind of evidence not only to validate his literary opinion
of Ghana's Ayi Kwei Armah, but, even more important, to demonstrate its superiority over the opinion of Ghanaian intellectuals' (p. 6).
Achebe continues with another example: 'In his book, *The Emergence
of African Fiction* [1972], Charles Larson tells us a few revealing things
about universality. In a chapter devoted to Lenrie Peters' novel which
he finds particularly impressive he speaks of "its universality, its very
limited concern with Africa itself"' (p. 8). Then he continues, quoting
from my book, to explain his argument:

> 'That it is set in Africa appears to be accidental, for except for a few
> comments at the beginning, Peters' story might just as easily take
> place in the southern part of the United States or, in the southern
> regions of France or Italy. If a few names of characters and places
> were changed one would indeed feel that this was an American novel.
> In short, Peters' story is universal.'

But Larson is obviously not as foolish as this passage would make
him out to be, for he ends it on a note of self-doubt which I find
totally disarming. He says:

> 'Or am I deluding myself in considering the work universal? Maybe
> what I really mean is that *The Second Round* is to a great degree
> Western and therefore scarcely African at all.'

I find it hard after that to show more harshness than merely agree-
ing about his delusion. But few people I know are prepared to be so
charitable. In a recent review of the book in *Okike*, a Nigerian critic,
Omolara Leslie, mocks 'the shining faith that we are all Americans
under the skin'.

Does it ever occur to the Larsons of African literature to try out
their game of changing names of characters and places in an American novel, say, a Philip Roth or an Updike, and slotting in African
names just to see how it works? But of course it would not occur to
them. It would never occur to them to doubt the universality of their

own literature. In the nature of things the work of a Western writer is automatically informed by universality. It is only others who must strain to achieve it. So and so's work is universal; he has truly arrived! As though universality were some distant bend in the road which you may take if you travel out far enough in the direction of Europe or America, if you put adequate distance between you and your home. I should like to see the word *universal* banned altogether from discussions of African literature until such a time as people cease to use it as a synonym from the narrow, self-serving parochialism of Europe, until their horizon extends to include all the world. (pp. 8–9)[1]

The appropriation of African literature by non-African scholars has taken on differing permutations, whether it be the connections I have drawn between African and western literary works (and the concept of universality, which I also believe is problematic), the attempts by Bernth Lindfors to see that important manuscripts by African writers are protected in appropriate archival collections, or, even more recently, the harsh statements by Wole Soyinka against James Gibbs, whom he accuses of appropriating his life, since for years Gibbs has been collecting information about the Nobel Prize Laureate, presumably for a biography.

I raise these issues and examples because they involve complicated issues of which most of us are unaware when we move between cultures. I have certainly drawn erroneous conclusions, and therefore interpretations, about aspects of African (and other) cultures when I have written about their literary works. I am aware that I am regarded as part of the problem. To a certain extent, all critics appropriate (or at least borrow) a literary text when they write anything about it – even a totally positive criticism. The situation is more complicated, however, when living writers are involved, bridging two or more cultures. A contemporary writer is entitled to say, 'Larson doesn't know what he is talking about', or, 'Larson's judgements are filtered through western eyes' (i.e. Larson is not African enough). Legitimate statements.

---

1. An even stronger response to what I have written about African literature came from Ayi Kwei Armah, who accused me of 'larsony' ('Larsony, or Fiction as Criticism of Fiction').

In spite of the recent trend towards greater cultural awareness and cultural diversity, there has been a narrowing in the academy in the past two decades, with some writers and critics asserting that only African Americans should write about or teach African American literature, that only women should write about or teach women's literature, that only Africans should be involved with African literature, and so on. These issues have been debated continuously at academic conferences and in scholarly journals. I understand how these positions have evolved and know that in the case of African writers I, too, would probably respond similarly if the situation were reversed. Ngugi wa Thiong'o is correct: cultural imperialism is not something imaginary, it is real. African writers have not been free to write and publish what they want without confronting western constructs and assumptions. Still, I would like to believe that in some small way my work has been more beneficial than harmful to African writers. Certainly, for many years when I reviewed African literary works for western periodicals, I knew that if I did not review a given work, it would probably be ignored.

Chinua Achebe and I have been friends for some time. He knows that my ideas about Africa and African writers have evolved since those naïve assertions expressed about certain passages of *The Emergence of African Fiction*. Ayi Kwei Armah, whom I have never met, is no doubt unhappy that I continue to write about African writers, that the field today (twenty-five years after he first wrote his essay) is not that much different. The reviewers of African literary works in American publications still tend to be Americans. English critics still tend to dominate the reviews of these works in British publications. Certain aspects of publishing (including the limited coverage of African literature by Africans in the African press) continue to be intractable and are not likely to change significantly in the future.

I continue to believe that literature and the other arts bring us together rather than separate us. Perhaps this is an old-fashioned opinion to hold in these post-colonial days, but, regrettably, where the arts are concerned the post-colonial era has not been much of an improvement over the colonial era. For better or worse, we are all born into a specific body, a specific culture and a specific era. We read because we desire to understand something about others beyond our own immediate culture and era. We also read because we are all inescapably human and curious about what the rest of the world is like beyond the boundaries we ourselves have constructed but which, deep down, we know we must destroy.

Western scholarly interest in and 'appropriation' of African literary works may appear to the writers themselves to be not far removed from the other 'threats' or encroachments on their writing: censorship, forced exile, aborted literary careers, and death. In the last two years of his life, Ken Saro-Wiwa became what he had talked about for years: *l'homme engagé*, an intellectual man of action. He was not alone, particularly in Nigeria. Chinua Achebe published *The Trouble with Nigeria* in 1983; after Saro-Wiwa's death, Wole Soyinka published *The Open Sore of a Continent* (1996). These writers have siphoned off their energies from their creative works and turned to political commentary, which is only to say that the political situation in a number of African countries has become so deplorable that writers have felt compelled to write about politics instead of continuing with their imaginative works.

Censorship and forced exile have gone hand-in-hand with these publications, as they have in other countries (apartheid in South Africa; Banda's repression of artists in Malawi) for years. As we will shortly see, writers have seen their works banned; they have had their government positions taken away from them; they have fled their countries for fear of reprisals. Yet against all these odds – illiteracy; a highly fragmented reading audience; use of an imported language; disproportionate economic restrictions on all aspects of book production, as well as the limited purchasing power of most Africans; conflicting aesthetic responses to their work; censorship, forced exile and death – the writer in Africa has been very much a presence on the international literary scene for fifty years. Imagine for just a moment the shape of that world without African writers. Indeed, it would be a very different world. The loss would be incalculable.

CHAPTER 3

African Writers and the Quest for Publication

A writer must be willing to experiment, no matter what problems this might produce with a publisher. The publisher is concerned with selling, with finding a market, and an audience, usually the maximum market and audience. In all this, of course, a publisher might still be interested in nurturing the writer's own original voice, as mine has been. However, a writer's aim must be singular; the writer is interested in perfecting the art form. That is all. The rest must be left to chance and the good instinct of readers who will love the work which has been done. If it is indeed well done, it will be recognized. If not, this will still be good work which has been produced. I have been extremely fortunate as a writer and found both local and international readers. I write on themes which I believe strongly in. I love my community and my country. I am willing to learn, and everyday I learn something new. I like discovering something about writing which I did not know yesterday. I never compromise my effort. (Yvonne Vera, letter to author, 4 October 1998)

I sometimes envy writers in some other societies ... whose problems are not quite as acute as ours. (Wole Soyinka, *West Africa*, 18–24 July 1994)

§ WITHOUT the pioneers of African writing, our concept of twentieth-century world literature would, indeed, be very different from the one with which we are familiar. Yet even at the beginning of the twenty-first century, most educated readers outside the continent have little genuine understanding of Africa; it is an area of the world that is, unfortunately, still opaque, if not dark, to them. So, too, the continent's writers. Ask a university student in the United States to name an African writer, and the reply is almost always Chinua Achebe. In Europe, particularly France, the response may be extended to include Léopold Sédar Senghor, one of the fathers of *négritude*, though Senghor may be remembered more for his presidency of Senegal than for his poems. With the literate elite in Europe, a few additional names will probably be mentioned: Wole Soyinka, because he was the first African to be awarded the Nobel Prize, in 1986 (followed by the Egyptian Naguib Mahfouz, in 1988, and the South African Nadine Gordimer, in 1991). Since 1991, Ben Okri, a Nigerian, has been popular with British readers because of *The Famished Road*, which won the Booker Prize that year. And, more recently, the Somalian Nuruddin Farah, recipient of the Neustadt Prize for literature in 1998, would also no doubt be mentioned.

Add to this list Ngugi wa Thiong'o, Sembene Ousmane (though probably more for his films than for his novels), Amos Tutuola, Camara Laye, and possibly Cyprian Ekwensi and Es'kia Mphahlele, and then the names quickly run out. Feminists may have had limited exposure to Bessie Head, Ama Ata Aidoo, Tsitsi Dangarembga, Buchi Emecheta, and one or two others, though the numbers are still limited. The situation is akin to that of the ignorance of most educated Americans regarding African American writers until the 1970s. One hopes that it will not take as long for African writers to become as widely read as their African American brothers and sisters in the United States.

Yet somehow I doubt this. The population of sub-Saharan Africa is approximately 360 million people and yet those millions have only been able to support one writer, which is to say that only Chinua Achebe, by my estimate, would be in a position to live a comfortable life on the royalties from his writing. 'Would be' because Achebe is also an academic. Could the same be said of Wole Soyinka if he had not won the Nobel Prize? Without the Booker Prize and the Neustadt, would Ben Okri and Nuruddin Farah be able to survive solely on their writing income? Soyinka teaches from time to time and lectures extensively; Farah has held short-term teaching stints. Only Ben Okri has been free of the classroom.

Except for Ben Okri – the youngest of the writers mentioned here – few African writers in more recent years have been able to mould successful writing careers. The Booker Prize made that possible for

Okri. Until the arrival of the Caine Prize for African Writing in summer 2000, there were no such prestigious literary awards in Africa with a significant cash value to help the continent's eager writers. The Noma Award for Publishing in Africa, perhaps the continent's most important book prize, was funded by Kodansha Ltd, the Japanese Publishing House whose former chairman was Shoichi Noma. The Swedish literary award, the Voice of Africa, which includes a significant monetary component, was awarded to Yvonne Vera in 1999 for *Under the Tongue*. There are lesser awards – *all* awards are important if you are a writer – but they rarely include a monetary portion and are not likely to stimulate additional sales of a book in Africa as they often do in Europe and the United States. Much of this may change with the establishment of the Caine Prize for African Writing.

In an article ('In Once Literary Nigeria, "Things Fall Apart"') in the *Washington Post* (3 February 1996), Eniwoke Ibagere describes the realities of the recent literary culture in Nigeria, the African country that has produced more significant writers than any other and has the largest literate population capable of sustaining that literary climate. The prognosis is grim: many of the country's leading writers are in exile; Ken Saro-Wiwa was executed. Wole Soyina's *Ibadan – the Penkelemes Years*, his most recent book at the time, according to Ibagere, 'costs about 4,000 naira – more than the monthly salary of most civil servants'. The article continues, quoting Olayinka Solarin, president of the Nigerian Publishers' Association: 'Nigeria no longer has a big market for books and that is why books are scarce ... The economy is so battered that people think more of how to survive. Buying of books is only done when necessary. So publishers complain [that] they are left with no choice but to print very few copies.'

Soyinka's *Ibadan* was published in England. For their own publications, Nigerian publishers are described as having developed the 'book launch' to such a rarified state that some titles are for sale only at the launch and at vastly inflated prices. 'The best that many authors can hope for is a lavish launch ceremony, where the publisher runs off a limited edition that is snapped up by Nigeria's rich and powerful for inflated prices of up to 20,000 naira ($250) a copy.' Several years earlier, in an interview in *West Africa*, Wole Soyinka bemoaned the entire book launch practice: 'Launching culture has replaced publishing culture.' Copies at the 'launch' may never be available in bookstores. Do the elite even bother to read the books they have purchased at such prices? How do writers become read and known under such circumstances? Ibagere's article quotes Joop Berkhout, the publisher of Spectrum Books, for a remark he made about the country's bookstores: 'Books are hard to find in Nigeria because there are very few properly managed bookstores like we have abroad. You get cases of bookshops failing to pay after collecting books from publishers, who, naturally are unwilling to provide books free of charge.'

A more damning statement, also by Berkhout, is that 'Nigerians have a poor reading culture and seldom buy books.' If this is true of Nigeria, then what about the situation in other countries? In recent years, a steady litany of discouragement about African readers has been vocalized by writers across the continent. At a joint conference of African writers and publishers (the African Writers-Publishers Seminar) held in Arusha, Tanzania, 23–26 February 1998, Femi Oso-fisan and Dafe Otobo agreed that Africans 'do not go to bookstores'. Echoing a similar note during a panel discussion about African writing on National Public Radio (23 August 1997), when asked if he was read by his Gambian countrymen, Tijan M. Sallah confessed: 'Just a little bit among a few of the Gambian elite who can read and write. I think my work is much more known outside than inside [the country].' South African Sindiwe Magona responded similarly: 'I'm African. And people do not read my books. My books are well read and received at home by the white and coloured population groups.' The African elite do not 'put a lot of importance on reading and learning. And it's a shame because African writers write, I think, mainly to be read in Africa.'

African writers and educators have laid the blame on education systems (particularly in the early years), arguing that little emphasis is placed on reading. O. M. Lawal-Solarin has stated that 'few school children read for pleasure', but reading for pleasure requires suitable books. All too often the books that are available are imported, not written in the child's mother-tongue. James Tumusiime, the managing director of Fountain Publishers in Kampala, Uganda, provides the example of 'complete absence of children's books by Ugandan authors' until recently. Even though books currently exist, Tumusiime admits that 'children's books published locally in Uganda tend to be more expensive and yet less colourful than those published abroad.' One of the most widely respected publishers in Africa, Henry Chakava, has described his attempts to publish a series of children's books in Kenyan languages ('Children and Books: Kenya'). He commissioned texts from distinguished writers such as Ngugi wa Thiong'o and produced attractive books, using 'a generous layout, good paper and full colour illustrations on the cover and in the text'. Chakava's good intentions were thwarted by the realities of the market. 'After the initial five titles, I was unable to continue with this series because sales were poor. None of the books have been reprinted to this day.'

Chakava's intention of publishing children's books in African languages may have had only limited success but the series was followed by a much more successful line of children's books written in English. This series echoed Chinua Achebe's earlier call, during the 1987 Zimbabwe International Book Fair, that serious African writers save African children by writing 'at least two stories' suitable for them.[1] Currently, Chakava states that his company's 'children's publishing programme is the fastest growing part of our business and is likely to remain so for some time to come'. Speaking about the situation for such publishing in Nigeria, however, Chukwuemeke Ike, the Nigerian writer and president of the Nigerian Book Foundation, was not nearly so sanguine, though efforts have been made to instigate a nationwide Book Week, book forums and a Children's Book Day. At numerous book fairs, Zimbabwean educator Miriam Bamhare has made similar statements about the need for instilling a love of reading in children who should be trained in the 'celebration' of reading. Their teachers themselves may not be accustomed to read for pleasure; even librarians may fall into the same category. No wonder African writers, especially the younger ones who have yet to gain more than a toehold in publishing, are discouraged. Nowhere has this been brought home to me more explicitly than in the dozens of replies I received from writers across the continent in response to my questionnaire asking them to describe their publishing experiences.

---

1. Achebe himself has written and published books for children that have been successful in the Nigerian market (as well as having been published in Nigeria).

Pessimism and unhappiness are chronicled, often in elaborate detail, by many of these writers as they describe their encounters with African and European publishers. Some are naïve about the basic realities of publishing, perhaps even gullible, though to a certain extent this is true of writers everywhere. Nevilles Bsquared Oguohwo, a Nigerian, wrote about this naïvety in his response to the questionnaire: 'Most aspiring authors in Africa are lacking basic publishing information, though the advertising efforts of foreign publishers in the *Economist* magazine and others can be better referred to as quite captivating as they will always guarantee a manuscript to bookshelf and world wide sales service' (letter to author, 17 April 1998).

An unpublished Nigerian writer provided me with copies of his lengthy correspondence with the Minerva Press (a vanity press) in London. The acceptance letter, i.e. the 'Editorial Evaluation', refers to the author's novel as 'a concise, but substantial treatment of an important subject, unlike other books of its genre, it has that quality of pulling the readers in: instead of facing us with a deluge of facts and "dry" information, the investigation is dealt with through dialogue and interaction, which allows the reader to follow the investigation as though they were directly involved.' Ignoring the grammatical errors, one still detects a generic response that Minerva Press editors have made to hundreds if not thousands of writers. The letter continues: 'This is certainly an informed work, but it conveys information in an adequately digestible form; the style is precise, but lucid and "human" – the reader does not have to take notes in order to understand it. On the contrary, whilst being thoroughly objective in his undertakings, the author has preserved an essential sensitivity and empathy for its subject.' Then, in a separate letter, after the earlier acceptance of the book, the press's publishing terms are explained: the author will have to contribute £2800 if the book is published.

Vanity publishers in Britain and America generally operate in the same way. First, in answer to the initial query, the press admits its policy may involve the author contributing to production costs. After all, 'Many of the most successful writers began their careers by contributing to the cost of publishing their early work, including Mark Twain, Nathaniel Hawthorne, Lord Byron, Beatrix Potter, Edgar Allan Poe, A. A. Milne, Bernard Shaw, Marcel Proust, and of course Jane Austen. For economic reasons the large multinational groups who

dominate publishing worldwide very seldom take on new authors.'
Then, if a manuscript is submitted, the writer receives a letter of
acceptance – often for what is a mediocre book that no reputable
publisher would print. Finally, comes the letter asking for a financial
contribution that the writer probably does not realize is more than
enough to cover production costs and still make a tidy profit for the
press, since it is assumed that few copies of the book will ever be sold.

African writers may conclude from this that all publishers require
'contributions' from their writers. The writer who received these
letters from the Minerva Press stated in his letter to me that 'there is
no proper information about publishing' for Africans. How are they
to determine that an offer from a publisher is legitimate? Needless to
say, the £2800 requested would constitute a small fortune for almost
any African, which is perhaps a blessing. If the amount requested
could be met, the writer's loss would be genuine.

Such lack of knowledge about the machinations of publishing is
fully understandable given matters of distance (writers in Africa,
publishers in Europe) and culture (an assumption that a publisher in
England is reputable, honest). The larger issue, which extends well
beyond the domain of the vanity publishers, is that of a general lapse
of ethics among both African publishers and, to a lesser extent, their
European counterparts. In 1994, Cont Mhlanga suggested that the
biggest problem for an African writer is that he doesn't know what to
expect from a contractual agreement with a publisher: 'We need a
contract … to ensure minimum standards of ethics within the publishing industry and to help conscientise our writers.'

At the African Writers-Publishers Seminar held in Arusha in 1998,
many writers levelled accusations of unfair treatment at their publishers, though Kole Omotoso, like Cont Mhlanga earlier, attributed
the problem to a general 'innocence' among African writers. Taban lo
Liyong provided the example of the late Okot p'Bitek who 'sold the
manuscript of Song of Lawino for 200 Kenyan shillings outright',
though a renegotiation of his terms took place later. In more detail,
Niyi Osundare, a poet, spoke of 'having had eight publishers, of
whom only "two or three" sent royalty statements on a regular basis;
from one publisher, with whom he had published in 1983, he had
received no royalties to date'. When I wrote to him to request
additional details, Osundare replied: 'Of my eight publishers only one

is in Europe, and that one sends my royalty statements regularly. Two of my Nigerian publishers also send royalty statements, though one of them has a way of promising to pay "when the economy improves", as we say in Nigeria. The others have never deemed it fit to send any statements' (letter to author, 21 October 1998).

Other African writers describe instances in which publishers have conveniently forgotten to pay royalties on published books, which in many cases means that the writer has received no money, since, typically, there is no advance. Véronique Tadjo, from the Ivory Coast, had this to say about the subject: 'When and if you receive your royalties, the statement is always fairly vague. In fact, the surest thing is to go there in person and demand your due, which, as you can imagine, is a very unpleasant thing to have to do. Mind you, this is not special to L'Harmattan [the French publisher]. Most African publishers are the same. Royalties don't exist or are sporadic' (letter to author, 21 May 1997). In a remark about the same publishing house (regarded as the major Francophone publisher for Africans although it is based in Paris), Manthia Diawara told me that L'Harmattan pays no royalties on the first 1000 copies of a title (telephone conversation with author, 18 September 1998). Thus, if sales are poor, it would be easy for a writer who has forgotten the terms of the contract to conclude that L'Harmattan pays no royalties at all.

With terms and conditions such as these, the pessimism expressed by a number of writers in their response to the questionnaire is hardly surprising. Sanya Osha, from the Department of General Studies at Ladoke Akintola University of Technology in Nigeria, decided to title her response 'The End of Nigerian Literature?' Representative comments about European publishing houses include the following: 'The truth is that African writing is not the in-thing in several areas of the global cultural marketplace'; 'Publishing African writing … is no different from charity work'. In Nigeria, 'conventional publishing for creative writers can be said to have died'. Thus, 'self-publishing has become a necessity' but 'marketing those books must surely be a huge handicap. Similarly, upcoming authors face great editorial difficulties as they have to do virtually everything on their own. As it is now, most of those books merely circulate within literary circles instead of the larger public where they are probably more needed and where ultimately the writer is able to judge her full worth.'

Worse, mentioning both Roland Barthes and Michel Foucault, Osha refers to 'the death of the author', but in this case the metaphor applies to Nigerian authors. In these difficult times, she asks, 'How can you deconstruct what has not even been constituted? The post-colonial legacy has been one of needless tragedy on all fronts ... and still we struggling writers continue to shuffle to various nondescript publishing houses biting our fingernails for parting with borrowed money and for an endeavour that has all the likelihood of ending in oblivion' (letter to author, 24 September 1997).

Osha's Nigerian compatriot, Jekwu Ikeme, provides an equally negative account of trying to get a volume of his poems into print. One Nigerian publisher asked him point blank, 'Who reads poetry?' He tried several others both at home and abroad, and finally a publisher proposed that Ikeme contribute 75 per cent of the production costs, money he did not have. The publisher said he would not even have accepted the book except for the fact that it included a Foreword written by 'a renowned poet and playwright'. So Ikeme talked to more than thirty 'philanthropists', literally begging them to help him with the financial part of the venture. 'I even offered dedicating the work to anyone who is willing to fund the project, but yet no dice.' His current emotional state? 'Like every writer in Africa, I have become numb to shock and disappointment' (letter to author, 12 August 1997).

The malaise expressed by African writers about current publishing opportunities both at home and abroad permeates every aspect of publishing. The economies of many African countries have been so broken that, with a few notable exceptions, the publishing of imaginative works by their writers has ceased. Publishing houses that existed until recently, such as Baobab Books in Zimbabwe, were flooded with manuscripts and could publish only a fraction of them, no matter what their merit. Other African publishers have decided to cater to the educational market, in some cases editing out potentially offensive passages in novels, so that these works will be approved by their governments for the classroom. Writers identify several levels of this growing form of censorship. First, they themselves may not write what they would like because of the fear of repression by their governments. Their local publishers are likely to excise passages deemed offensive for sexual, political, and/or religious reasons. Even worse, publishers outside Africa fear repercussions for books that may be deemed politically incorrect, for a variety of reasons.

Writers thus see themselves as beleaguered on all sides. At the Arusha conference, Kole Omotoso identified the dangers of this current censorship from abroad: 'foreign readers too often refused to take on the issues of contemporary Africa, preferring outdated versions of Africa which suit their vested interests.' Agnes Sam, a South African Indian writer, has written about her difficulties in getting an experimental novel published:

> The original draft was impressionistic, its form suggestive of a fractured society, of people in an apartheid system isolated from each other. It combined poetry with prose. Its purpose was to frustrate the reader's need for continuity because this is precisely how we are frustrated in our understanding of the South African situation. I've seen other works published which are experimental and this reinforces my view that it isn't simply that the publishers determine what is acceptable for some prescribed market, but they have a stereotype of how one should write if belonging to a specific group. One publisher's representative asserted very firmly that black women write autobiographically. A black woman experimenting with language and form has no business writing. In the new Commonwealth, those writers who do not conform to these stereotypes are said to have been influenced by Western tradition, to have had an 'English' as opposed to a 'Bantu' or 'Third World' education, or they are said not to be writing for the 'people' ... But the crunch comes when we disregard Western tradition and publishers' stereotypes, and attempt to experiment – this isn't tolerated. (in Rosemary George, *The Politics of Home*, 1996, p. 119)

Ghanaian Ama Ata Aidoo has articulated similar thoughts about writing 'acceptable' literature for publishers outside the continent: 'someone can declare that your manuscript doesn't read like a manuscript from a third world person.' On another occasion, she spoke of the difficulties of being a woman writer: 'If it were not for the existence of feminist-controlled alternative presses, many works of creation and social criticism by women writers would not be published at all'. To which she added: 'It is a wonder women write at all.' Speaking to Lena Williams for the *New York Times* (22 October 1997), she said she was grateful that the Feminist Press at the City University of New York had published two of her books.

With so many negative comments about the state of publishing of African literature today, one wonders about the future prospects of the current generation of African writers. Excluding the *négritude* poets, the first generation of African writers – those who began publishing in the aftermath of the Second World War – mostly took the route of publishing in Europe, since that was almost the only path available to them. The second generation, beginning around 1970, had some successes with publishing in Africa but also frequently published their works overseas. One thinks of writers such as Ayi Kwei Armah, Ben Okri and Nuruddin Farah as some of the most popular writers in this generation, but, twenty or twenty-five years later, the economies of many African countries were in disarray and it became difficult for new writers to find receptive publishers. Even European publishers (Fontana and Heinemann, for example) were retrenching and publishing fewer works by African writers.

Where will African writers in the future find their publishers? Examining the careers of several writers – both those who have been successful and those who have not – will help us answer that question, though some of those writers have been attempting to assert their importance for more years than most writers are willing to endure.

Cyprian Ekwensi (Nigeria)

Writing a quarter of a century ago, Ernest Emenyonu, the Nigerian writer and critic, stated passionately of Cyprian Ekwensi: 'He has been praised and blamed but never correctly assessed as a writer. Critics who seem unable to cope with his versatility, not to mention his vast volumes, have abandoned him, and in effect his growth as a writer, which can be clearly discerned in a chronological study of his works, has been missed by many' (*Cyprian Ekwensi*, p. 3). Ekwensi is not only one of the most prolific African writers of the twentieth century but also a man who has had several different professional careers besides that of writer. An Ibo, he was born in 1921 in Northern Nigeria, but attended secondary school in Ibadan, in an area of the country that is predominantly Yoruba. His familiarity and apparent ease with several of his country's major ethnic groups have been reflected in his fiction.

Ekwensi's education continued in Ibadan (at Yaba Higher College) and then at Achimota College in Ghana. He studied forestry and worked for two years as a forestry officer. He also taught science courses briefly, worked for Radio Nigeria and, in 1949, entered the Lagos School of Pharmacy, subsequently continuing his studies at the University of London (Chelsea School of Pharmacy). During these years, Ekwensi also wrote his earliest fiction. He has frequently been identified as one of the major forces in the Onitsha Market Literature though his first book-length publication, *Ikolo the Wrestler and Other Ibo Tales* (1947), was published in London. When Ekwensi's ever-popular novel *Jagua Nana* (1961) was first published in the United States in 1969, the author listed nineteen books to his credit, beginning with *When Love Whispers* (1947).

Ernest Emenyonu identifies the significance of *When Love Whispers*: 'This short, light romance was one of the earliest works of fiction in English in Nigeria and may have helped to inspire the popular (Onitsha) pamphlet literature' (p. 7). Unlike other Nigerian writers, Cyprian Ekwensi made the transition from writing for readers of Onitsha Market Literature to a mainstream audience. Stated another way, Ekwensi discovered quite early in his career that there were Nigerians who could be lured into reading if there was suitable material to attract their attention. *When Love Whispers*, *Jagua Nana* and several of the writer's subsequent works mine the field of western popular fiction: sex, violence (though never as extreme as in the West), intrigue and mystery in a recognizable contemporary setting, more frequently than not in the fast-paced melting pot of the big city. To all this, Ekwensi has further added a relentless fascination with African women – in short, his works contain all the elements of western bestsellerdom, except that in recent years the concept of the bestseller in the Nigerian book market has been eclipsed by the country's depressed economy.

Both *When Love Whispers* and *Jagua Nana* focus upon a highly attractive Nigerian woman with multiple suitors. In the first novel, the conflict is brought about because Ashoka believes she has already discovered the love of her life, while her father expects her to marry a much older man in an arranged marriage. Jagua Nana is older and much more worldly: a forty-five-year-old prostitute, with a steady boyfriend in addition to her paying customers. This novel – like so many of the early Onitsha novels – shows us the seedy underbelly of the big city, in this case Lagos. Jagua's favourite haunt, the Tropicana bar, sets the scene for much of the story:

> All the women wore dresses which were definitely undersize, so that buttocks and breasts jutted grotesquely above the general contours of the bodies. At the same time the midriffs shrunk to suffocation. A dress succeeded if it made men's eyes ogle hungrily in this modern super sex-market. The dancers occupied a tiny floor, unlighted, so that they became silhouetted bodies without faces and the most un-athletic man could be drawn out to attempt the improvisation which went by the name *High-life*. (p. 14)

Jagua Nana was so popular in the 1960s that a film version was planned by an Italian movie company. The mere idea that a film of this sensational novel might provide the world with an unflattering glimpse of life in Nigeria led to discussions in the Nigerian Parliament that resulted in an abrupt cancellation of the project. Emenyonu notes the irony of this incident because it happened almost at the same time as Ekwensi was awarded the Dag Hammarskjöld International Prize in Literature (1968). This ironic juxtaposition is important because Ekwensi has written just as many 'literary' works as sensational ones, though he is more often remembered for the latter. Of his early books, *The Drummer* Boy (1960), *Passport of Mallam Ilia* (1960), *Burning Grass* (1962) and *Iska* (1966) are all 'serious' novels, some produced by academic publishers (such as Cambridge University Press) for the African market, and becoming set texts for the West African School Certificate examinations. There has always been this pull in Ekwensi's writing between the sensational and the serious, the playful and the concerned.

Cyprian Ekwensi has written hundreds of short stories, radio and television scripts, several dozen novels, including children's works, yet in the 1970s he said that his writing had brought him both fame and poverty. In response to my questionnaire, and perhaps in the mellowing of age, he wrote: 'Five decades or more of writing novels, novellas, short stories, children's books, have brought me world fame but not fortune. If I were an American living in America or Europe, I would be floating in a foam bath in my own private yacht off the coast of Florida' (letter to author, 8 March 1999).

Like many of his peers, Ekwensi agrees that the reading culture of his country (and of the continent) has changed drastically during the course of his fifty-year career. Even more extreme changes have taken place in the world of publishing. When he began writing in the days of Onitsha Market Literature, 'the books came out spontaneously and unsolicited. They were hawked and distributed quickly. In many cases the Author was also the Publisher.' Books often sold quite well; several of his most successful Onitsha publications were reprinted frequently. Today, 'There is rigid control by the publishers (and by the economy). Your book has to fit into their schedules and programmes and not the other way around. Radio and TV and, lately, video have destroyed the reading culture.' What little reading there is, is chiefly of set texts within the schools.

Ekwensi especially bemoans the state of 'big business' publishing, which has altered the entire context of writing for the author:

> There are big African publishers with Foreign Partners and there are Nigerian publishers on their own and there are aspiring author self-publishers. The objective of all of them is to sell books, but it is more lucrative to have as your customer the World Bank Project or the Ministry of Education or the Petroleum Trust Fund. These conglomerates place large orders and some authors, especially of textbooks, benefit by the bulk sums paid in royalties. Always bear in mind that publishing is a business. The smaller publisher of creative books is a retailer whose returns will not pay the rent for the author's one-bedroom apartment, much less buy him a decent *agbada* for the family ceremonials. But his friends have by now heard that he has become an 'author' and that is a feather in his cap.

Of the 'book launch' that Soyinka and others have so decried, Ekwensi states that the publisher with enough clout can 'rake in thousands of naira by way of recouping investments. The money is shared as per agreement but this system fails to provide regular income for the writer.' Writers, typically, have to sign contracts 'loaded in favour of the publisher', granting them control of world rights which they are 'incapable of selling or enforcing'. Authors seldom receive royalties from their books without demanding them: 'I have yet to know of an African author *living in Africa* who died a wealthy man from his writing. The rich ones all live abroad.'

Perhaps the major problem that Ekwensi identifies is an attitude towards the creative writer himself/herself:

> Writing is still regarded not as a career but as a charitable pursuit – designed to educate and entertain readers with nothing coming to the writer. The mention of money appears obscene, but the glamour is there and thousands do take the plunge, but support it with moonlighting or chasing jobs in construction companies or Ministries. As for writing being a career, the writer will have to try the Media – especially radio, television and the regular press. Journalists thrive there, but creative writers get diverted and the creativity gets washed out of them if they must take the bread and butter home. Ending up in the gulag of some dictatorial government is just one of the hazards of the trade.

Ekwensi none the less has kind words to say about Spectrum Books, in Ibadan, which published one of his more recent novels, *Jagua Nana's Daughter* (1986). My conversations with Joop Berkhout, the publisher, revealed that current sales of the novel total a couple of thousand copies a year – in a country once considered to be full of readers (interview, 6 August 1998).

Except for those years when he studied pharmacy in England, Ekwensi has remained a Nigerian writer living in Nigeria. He supports himself by his profession as a pharmacist, yet still he keeps writing, moving with the times (when I talked to him recently, he enthusiastically described a short story he had published on the Internet). In his response to my questionnaire, he identified himself as 'one of the pioneers of modern African writing'. No one in the field of African literature would question that. Still, I can't help wondering whether, if he had his writing career to begin all over again, he might not consider the expatriate route of so many of his contemporaries:

> Living abroad, the African writer is then in the midst of publishers, booksellers, world writers and others who respond to his presence and give him his due place in society. He even becomes an Ambassador of African cultures, which is as it should be. Communication is speedy and efficient and all the world becomes a stage on which he can play his part. Even so, the Exile is homesick, out of touch and is

only postponing the evil date when he will come home and find he has become irrelevant.

It's a dog's life.

It is impossible to determine the antecedent of the pronoun in the concluding statement: the African writer in exile – or all African writers?

Similih M. Cordor (Liberia)

The successes that have been part of Cyprian Ekwensi's literary career can only be imagined by Liberian writer Similih M. Cordor. Cordor was born in Voinjama, in northern Liberia, in 1946, and has suffered almost all the indignities that can be inflicted upon a writer, largely because of his Liberian heritage. As Liberians are wont to say, their country did not enjoy the benefits of colonialism. Instead, Liberia – founded by freed American slaves in 1822 – was largely abandoned by the United States (except for the exploitation of its natural resources by American companies) once the cursory repatriation of ex-slaves was facilitated.

The jokes about Liberia's culture are legion. Cordor says: 'For nearly a century and a half, Liberia had no genuinely regarded authentic national literature, music, painting, or sculpture' (letter to author, 27 July 1997). The repatriated slaves, who were largely un-educated, dominated the indigenous tribes, each group looking down on the other, though the Ameri-Africans continued to control the country politically until the coup of 1980. Cordor has described himself as growing up in a cultural vacuum, wanting not only to be a writer but also a catalyst for an artistic revolution in his country. He says his decision to become a writer

> emerged out of my deep conviction that Liberia, which had played an important political role in African history … should also play a significant role in modern African literature. I felt that Liberia had to be an important part of the contemporary African writings that had risen after the demise of European colonialism on the African continent. But this was not going to be an easy task because my country had no rich literary traditions.

As an aspiring writer, Cordor quickly discovered that there were no book publishers in his country, and even very few printers. American publishers to whom he sent his manuscripts had no interest in Liberian literature, and English publishers were not interested in him because he wasn't from a former British colony. Liberia, in fact, has had few links with other African countries, certainly none of them cultural. There was a general 'disdain for indigenous African cultures' among the descendants of the American slaves. They 'despised African ways of life' and tried to imitate American life instead. Book-reading among the middle class was virtually unknown, except for imported textbooks used in the schools.[2]

Cordor wanted to change all this. His initial problem was determining how he was going to get published. He talked to people in the Ministry of Education, hoping that they would be interested in the short stories he was writing, since they were about Liberian characters and situations, but, after reading them, 'Officials in the ministries complained about the content of my short stories and decided against publishing them'. This was his first *de facto* encounter with censorship. He sent his work to publishers in Ghana and Nigeria, but either the manuscripts were lost or the publishers wanted subsidies beyond the means of his teacher's salary. Thus, he made the decision to publish his own work.

Initially, these works (his own short stories and quasi-critical works, *A Guide to the Study of Liberian Literature*, 1971, and *Towards the Study of Liberian Literature*, 1972) were mimeographed and stapled together. He refers to himself in those days as 'a one-man research organization', though he was assisted by his students at Monrovia College (the secondary school where he taught). Almost immediately he discovered a ready-made audience, suggesting that Liberians had simply been waiting for someone to produce imaginative materials by and about them. These books quickly sold out and had to be reprinted. 'Readers liked my stories because the themes were uniquely Liberian, and Liberians could see themselves, their lives, and the patterns of Liberian culture in my fictional dramatization of Liberian societal and cultural nuances.'

In 1977, he produced his most successful work, *Modern West African*

---

2. About the only Liberian literary work ever mentioned is Bai T. Moore's *Murder in the Cassava Patch* (1968).

Stories from Liberia, the first anthology of his country's short stories to be published locally. Most of the copies were immediately purchased for courses at the University of Liberia. Other works soon followed. 'I soon found out that Liberians were ready to read.' The problem was that there were few books by other writers for them to read. Then, just as it looked as if Cordor might become his country's first true writer/publisher, things fell apart. Under Samuel Doe, the army staged one of the most ruthless coups that the continent has seen. Cordor had already branched out into political commentary, having quickly produced *National Reconstruction for a New Liberia* (1979) during the period of growing instability leading up to the coup, and then *Liberia under Military Rule* (1980), after the coup, both mimeographed booklets. He had also linked up with a printer in the United States who published for him *Africa, from People to People* (1979), another collection of short stories, and *Facing the Liberian Nation* (1980). As one of his country's leading intellectuals, he began to fear for his life, though he admits that the Tolbert regime that preceded Doe's had also been repressive.

> Over the years many writers, journalists, and teachers found them-
> selves in trouble and got arrested, detained, or imprisoned for their
> writings that were critical of the government or political leaders. Both
> civilian and military regimes were equally harsh in the treatment of
> writers and journalists, though the military rulers were much more
> ruthless in dealing with 'dissident voices of the intelligentsia.' And I
> was no exception.

Cordor himself 'suffered intimidation, harassment, and detention for being critical of the government and political leaders'. He had had his first run-in with the government back in 1972 when he was a student at the University of Liberia. More serious problems began in 1979, still before the coup, when he was arrested while invigilating an examination of his students at Monrovia College. He was taken to the Executive Mansion, questioned about his writings, and then released. Arrested again (his apartment was searched and some of his writings were confiscated), he was taken to the headquarters of the National Security Agency and detained for a day. Cordor was accused of trying to foment a revolution in the country. Finally, fearing the repressive Doe government after the coup, he decided to accept a fellowship to pursue graduate work in the United States, funded by the University of Liberia. The government may have considered this an easy way to silence him.

Cordor refers to his state of 'mental turmoil, political disillusionment' when he left Liberia. Graduate work in English was challenging, but it interrupted his writing. He might have been more comfortable in a creative writing programme or one in publishing. 'I felt depressed because my writing slowed down. I wanted to write, but each time I delved deeper into my writing, my studies suffered; and, conversely, each time I put much work into my PhD studies, my writing career suffered. I felt trapped, dismayed, and saddened.' His wife and children were in Liberia; he feared for their lives. More than anything else, he felt severed from his roots, his culture, even though he continued to be harassed by Liberian government officials in the United States. As he says of these years:

> I was having nightmares about the notorious and despicable ways the soldiers were ruining the country. I tried to concentrate on my graduate studies but I could not. I was very impatient; I wanted to return home quickly to continue my writing. I felt that the most important materials for my fiction, poetry, drama, and nonfiction works were in Liberia. As a cultural nationalist, I feel that my soul is tied to the soul of my country. I glory in the cultural heritage of my society and I shine in the historical depth of my country. I sing the songs of my people; I sing the songs they are afraid to sing because of the sociopolitical atmosphere of our society. I journey into the national psyche of my country to search for materials for my writing; I am a child of my country. So I wanted to be back home as soon as possible, but this was never to happen as I hoped for. After sixteen years I am still living abroad in exile.

The sixteen years have stretched beyond that. During these years, Cordor was joined in the United States by his wife and children, though he was unable to attend funerals of other members of his family. He accumulated extensive debts since his funds were cut off by the Liberian government shortly after he arrived in the USA. His PhD, delayed by innumerable teaching stints to pay the bills, was finally awarded in 1997. At times he was unemployed, bankrupt. Describing the years of exile in his elaborate response to my questionnaire, he used such terms and phrases as: 'I felt terribly helpless'; 'I felt that I had let my people down as a writer'; 'I felt depressed that I was not at home to witness the war first hand and write about it'; 'I sank into a deep writer's block. My mind dried up and lost its concentrative power'; 'I felt my life exploding and breaking into two separate worlds: (1) My world before the war, and (2) My world after the war'.

Finally, at about the time he finished his PhD, he stated 'the war forced me to realize that I was now in exile for good'. The only thing he had to return to was his writing. In part he reached this state by writing poetry, a genre he had not pursued before. 'My Past, My Present, My Future' talks candidly about his current state:

> I have put all my past behind me;
> it is lying over the hills of Voinjama,
> deep down in the heart of Lofa in Liberia.
> I am singing my past over my bygone years
> because it has become my historical self.
> I have translated my past into my yesterday.
>
> I have put all my present before me;
> it is lying in the anguish of my exile,
> far, far away from my people in Liberia.
> My present is all I have at the moment
> and I am trying to live it now.
> I have spread my present over my today.
>
> I have put all my future ahead of me;
> it is awaiting the day I return home,
> all the way to my native land in Liberia.
> My future is going to be mine someday
> I can see it approaching very soon.
> I have ear marked my future for my tomorrow.

In the covering letter to his lengthy response to my questionnaire, Similih M. Cordor takes an upbeat approach to his exiled status in the United States but is still concerned about the 'question of a genuine national literature in Liberia', the focus of much of his energy for nearly thirty years. With bittersweet recognition, he adds: 'I kind of feel depressed that I do not have great published novels, poems, and plays to my name to show for all these many years that

I have been trying to become a writer from Liberia.' Yet he also acknowledges the stability of his current life:

> I now have a full-time teaching job with good benefits and a not bad salary ... I have managed to deal with many difficult personal and family matters that had been eating deep into my psyche. I still grieve over my people and homeland and I still experience the anguish of exile, but I am now much better off – mentally, physically, and spiritually – than half a decade ago. I have taken care of my painful experiences like unemployment and its devastating financial turmoil, debts to the IRS, eviction from apartments, bankruptcy, repossession of my cars, assault on my self-esteem, debts to friends and relatives, and the depressive illnesses that accompanied all these terrible experiences.

Véronique Tadjo (Ivory Coast)

Although she writes in French, Véronique Tadjo has relied on her own translations into English to ensure the quality of her work. Fortunately, her cosmopolitan education and professional career have provided her with fluency in both languages. Born in Paris in 1955, she grew up in Abidjan, in the Ivory Coast, where she attended local schools. Her BA in English was awarded by the University of Abidjan, followed by a doctorate in African American Literature and Civilization from the Sorbonne. She taught at the University of Abidjan in the early 1980s, though she spent part of 1983 in Washington, DC, at Howard University, on a Fulbright fellowship. While holding various teaching positions in those years, she also began writing both poetry and prose (including children's books).

She describes her early writing career as successful, but says that the frustrations of the market have intervened in recent years. She is not the first to admit that writers in many countries – particularly in England and the United States – can often relate unsettling stories about their publishing. *Latérite*, her first volume of poems, was published in 1983, largely because she won first prize in a literary competition, the Prix de l'Agence de Coopération Culturelle et Technique. When she received a telephone call from Hatier, a well-known publisher of Francophone African writers, she was especially pleased because Hatier had recently initiated an African writers series called 'Monde Noir Poche'. According to Tadjo, the titles in the series 'were sold at an affordable price and well-distributed' (letter to author, 21 May 1997). *Latérite* became the first volume of poems in the series, and it received especially favourable attention from the media in Abidjan. 'This experience proved to me that poetry when well marketed can become very popular, contrary to what most publishers say.'

After *Latérite*, Tadjo wrote an experimental novel called *A vol d'oiseau* (*As the Crow Flies*). Its dozens of short chapters can be read as self-contained short stories (and a number of them have been published as such), but when read together they form an unconventional novel. Tadjo received the impression that Hatier was not interested in publishing the work, but that was a misunderstanding. By the time she realized this she had already begun searching for another publisher. A publisher in Senegal told her that the book was too depressing, but Fernand Nathan, a French publisher known for its textbooks, accepted the book because it was beginning an African literature series. For the second time, Tadjo says, one of her books received a great amount of attention.

Unfortunately, shortly after *A vol d'oiseau* (1989) was published, Fernand Nathan merged with Larousse and the new series was abruptly abandoned, after only five titles had appeared. 'As writers, we had to fight for our rights because the publisher expected us to accept our fate without any discussion. A few of us got together and through pressure made them pay royalties on all the books which were going to be destroyed (without our knowledge).' Thus ended Véronique Tadjo's honeymoon with her publishers. That year, she says, she received a significant amount of money from royalties, but once again she had to look for another publisher. And the life of *A vol d'oiseau* was abruptly cut short because no other publisher wanted to reprint it.

Deciding where to publish next – in Africa or in France – became a time-consuming endeavour. Eventually, she decided on L'Harmattan, again in France. 'My choice was due to the fact that Ivorian publishing was in a bad state after the financial collapse of the two main government-owned local publishers. The situation was more or less the same elsewhere on the continent. To publish in Africa would have meant to be confined within the borders of the country from where the publisher in question operated. It also meant the risk of having an editing job that wasn't satisfying.' As an example, she says that she gave a new volume of her poems to Les Nouvelles Éditions du Sénégal, 'who were among the rare ones to publish poetry. They did such a bad job (mistakes plus bad layout) that I had to refuse to accept the book, and since they made the mistake of sending me the contract after publication, I refused to sign it.'[3]

In 1992, L'Harmattan published Tadjo's second novel, *Le Royaume Aveugle (The Blind Kingdom)*. The results were less than satisfying. Tadjo felt that the publishing house was simply too big to offer any personal attention. 'The book comes out quickly, yes. But your work is lost in a multitude of other books of uneven quality. Just one visit in their bookshop will give you an idea of what their publishing company is like: it is total chaos! So many books everywhere that you can hardly move around, while you wonder how they find anything.' There was no advertising and no review copies were sent to the media. Worse, 'Their books are very expensive for the African market.' And writers, she adds, often accuse L'Harmattan of dishonesty: 'One of my good friends told me that one day, while on a trip to Italy for a workshop, he saw a translation of his novel in Italian. And he didn't even know about it!' He now wants to take them to court. To receive her own royalties, Tadjo had to go to L'Harmattan's offices and demand to be paid.

Despite these problems, Tadjo is encouraged to keep writing by the positive criticism she has received. Her work has been reprinted in numerous anthologies; she has been invited to international conferences. Other writers and critics have given her 'good feedback. They encourage me to continue in the difficult path that I have chosen.' Still, in 1997, she bemoaned her current situation, commenting:

> I would very much like to find a publisher whom I trust and with whom I can discuss my work and its direction. Will this publisher be in Europe or in Africa? I don't really know. The situation back home [in Francophone Africa] is still not great although since the devaluation of the CFA franc, things have changed. It has given a boost to local

---

3. The Nigerian poet Niyi Osundare suffered an even worse indignity when one of his publishers, in Nigeria, made a miscalculation. To solve the problem of lack of space, the typesetter simply ran all the lines of the poems together, setting them as prose instead of verse.

publishers because imported books have become far too expensive for the majority of the people. Consequently, books are now produced locally. It goes without saying that school books are the priority. Fortunately, publishers are slowly taking an interest in literature. But the know-how still lacks professionalism and the problem of distribution still remains.

She says she is particularly encouraged by Les Nouvelles Éditions Ivoiriennes, recently privatized, which publishes children's books, including her own.

A collection of Tadjo's poems, *A mi-chemin*, which she wrote several years ago, was scheduled to be published by Feu de Brousse, but has never appeared. The publisher, she notes, 'seems to have disappeared from the earth ... And to think that I had corrected the proofs! The sad thing is that it has made me lose several years. It has almost made me give up on poetry. Luckily, I am a poet at heart and will always find ways of getting it out' (e-mail to author, 26 February 1999).

Tadjo notes that the ideal publishing situation for her would be joint publication: an edition for the European and American market, priced at one rate, and an edition for the African market, priced much more modestly. 'It would be the best of both worlds, as I am writing primarily for an African audience but also for anyone else who enjoys reading' (letter to author, 21 May 1977). Her new novel, *Champs de bataille et d'amour*, will be published under this kind of arrangement by Présence Africaine in Paris and Nouvelles Editions Ivoiriennes, 'which means that the African market will be satisfied and the European one as well' (e-mail to author, 26 February 1999).

Reflecting on publishing in general for the African writer, Tadjo remarks:

It is a difficult business where talent is not enough. You need determination, endurance and courage. You have highs and lows, victories and failures but if you are ready to fight for it and if you believe in yourself, I think there is still room for more writers in African publishing. The important thing is to develop the African market in order to make African publishing a viable enterprise.

About her own writing, Tadjo has stated:

I write because I want to understand the world I'm living in, and because I want to communicate with others my experience of what it is to be living in Africa today. I use my eyes like a camera, trying to record everything, from the most personal emotions to the major crises like wars, death, and AIDS. When asked what my novels are about, I sigh heavily and say, 'About life,' because I cannot explain it in any other way. I am interested in life in its entirety, and this is why I have an aversion to giving names to my characters. I want the readers to see them as human beings first of all. And these human beings are faced with challenges and struggles they must overcome if they want to retain their humanity in the unfavorable context of an African society in crisis. (quoted in Larson, *Under African Skies*, p. 277)

Elinor Sisulu (Zimbabwe/South Africa)

Elinor Sisulu, author of children's books, was born in Salisbury (Harare), in Rhodesia (Zimbabwe) in 1958. When asked by children today if she first decided to be a writer when she was a child, she responds:

I would have been considered completely mad. The horizons of a black child growing up in Rhodesia in the 1960s were very limited. Successful people in our society were either teachers or nurses. Those who set their sights high could aspire to be lawyers or doctors, but a writer? Never. This was something completely outside our experience. As for a writer of children's books, this was something quite unheard of. (letter to author, 9 October 1998)

Nevertheless, at school, Sisulu showed a talent for writing, prompting her when somewhat older to consider journalism as a career. She was warned, however, that 'journalism was reckless, dangerous, and an unreliable occupation, so I quickly put the idea away until I grew up'. The books she read as a child 'were about the English countryside. My head was filled with a vision of snow, goblins and pixies.' Her favourite writers were Charles Dickens, Enid Blyton and Richmal Crompton.

If I came across Africa at all in the course of my reading, it was in the stories about missionaries, explorers and exotic jungles – nothing to do with my own reality. My own culture and society was never reflected in the printed word. Perhaps this is why the idea of being a writer was so alien in our society. Books were about a differing and exciting world. I would never have dreamed of writing about my own experiences or of those of people around me – I thought my own world was too boring and mundane.

At the University of Zimbabwe in Harare beginning in 1976, Sisulu studied English and history and was also introduced to African literature. After graduation, she worked for the government in the Ministry of Manpower Planning and Development. In 1985, she took a leave from her job to pursue an MA in Development Studies at the Institute of Social Studies at The Hague. There she was introduced to feminist ideology. The following year she married Max Sisulu, a South African exile who worked for the African National Congress (ANC). Shortly thereafter, they moved to Lusaka, Zambia, where they both continued to work for the ANC. They were able to move to South Africa in 1991, following the social and political changes that would culminate in the end of apartheid.

About the same time, Sisulu began writing more imaginative material than the academic research she had been producing. For a brief period, she worked for *Speak*, a South African 'feminist magazine for black working class and rural women'. Then she received a Ford Foundation grant to write a joint biography of her in-laws, the South African leaders Walter and Albertina Sisulu. The grant took her to Radcliffe College for several months in 1993, but the major event that led to her first children's book grew out of South Africa's first democratic elections in April 1994.

Sisulu says that as a student in 1980 she had observed her own country's democratic elections and felt the excitement of that extraordinary period. Thus, the election in South Africa fourteen years later was the second occasion during which she observed history being made. The incident that inspired her occurred when she was working at one of the polling booths:

A shabbily dressed old man came to vote on the last morning of the election. Because the photograph on his tattered identity document was so worn out that his image was unrecognizable, the document could not be considered a valid form of identity. With heavy hearts, we had to explain to him that the only way he could vote was to get a temporary registration document at the Home Affairs office in the city center. It was painful to witness his disappointment as he turned away, bitter disappointment written all over his face. We knew he was unlikely to return – there was no public transport to town because the election days had been declared public holidays. Even if he did manage to get there, the queues of people trying to get temporary identity documents were several kilometers long.

By five thirty in the afternoon, there was just a trickle of voters coming in. The polling booth was virtually empty and the staff had started to pack up. The presiding officer had taken out the box of chocolates she had brought as a reward for the last voter. Five minutes before closing time, the old man hobbled in, triumphantly waving his temporary registration card! He had managed to walk all the way to town, queue for several hours for his card and walk all the way back with a few minutes to spare. It was hard to tell who was happier, the voter or the polling officers. We jumped back to attention and put him through the steps of the voting process. When he cast his ballot, the presiding officer presented him with his box of chocolates while another officer photographed him. Overjoyed and bewildered by the unexpected moment of celebrity, he acknowledged the rousing applause of the polling booth staff. We applauded with relief. For us the incident symbolized the incredible spirit and determination of the voters and justified the three days of arduous work at our little polling booth.

The children's book that grew out of this incident was *The Day Gogo Went to Vote*, published in the United States in 1996. Initially, a television company asked Sisulu to write her account of what she had seen during the voting. Once it was written, she showed her story to a visiting American friend, and that friend took a copy back to the States and gave it to an editor at Little, Brown. The book was quickly accepted, an illustrator was found, and both American and British editions were published. *The Day Gogo Went to Vote* was frequently cited as one of the most significant children's books of the year and won both the Best Children's Book Award of the African Studies Association and the Jane Adams Award for books promoting peace and democracy. Sales in the United States have subsequently reached 22,000 copies. The following year, Tafelberg Publishers in

South Africa released the book in six languages: Zulu, Xhosa, Sotho, Sepedi, Tswana and Afrikaans.

Sisulu states that as a writer of children's literature, she has been concerned about the decline of oral storytelling in African societies. 'If our stories are not written down and at the same time they are no longer being perpetuated through our oral traditions, they will disappear completely and in the process we will lose a valuable part of our history.' She admits that part of her desire to write for children was intensified by thinking of her own children. Although she has made sure that they have had access to children's literature, 'There is still a dearth of contemporary stories set in their own environment. I decided that I should write the kind of stories that I should have been able to read when I was a child.' She defines her goal as 'preserving history'. About *The Day Gogo Went to Vote*, she states: 'I have been able to express my feelings about the way the elderly are treated and valued in our society, to celebrate the special relationship between grandparents and grandchildren and to transmit a very special part of our history to future generations.'

It is no surprise that Elinor Sisulu holds strong opinions about the need for children's literature in African societies. But if books are too expensive for most Africans to buy, illustrated books (the kind she knows that children need) are even more so. Bookshops, she fears, will not stock them, if they cost too much. Thus, the very kinds of books most suitable for establishing reading patterns among children become even more problematic than books for adults. Nor do African teachers see the need for such imaginative works, which are often perceived by educators as 'supplementary' reading. 'Many teachers do not read widely and consequently do not use children's literature in the classroom. Teachers tend to focus on the mechanical act of reading and writing and not on using the story as a means to educate. Many teachers are not even aware that there is a substantive body of indigenous children's literature.'

In part to promote her book, but also to return to the city of her birth, Sisulu attended the Zimbabwe International Book Fair in Harare in August 1998. She thought it would be nice to visit the primary school she had attended as a child and talk about her book and her career as a writer. Her plan backfired, however, because she had not anticipated the bureaucratic obstacles that would prevent her visit.

On 5 August *The Herald* reported that the headmaster of Moffat Primary School had 'told her that she could not be allowed to see the pupils unless she was cleared by the Ministry of Education, Sport and Culture' ('Former Student Barred from Seeing Pupils at Old School'). Sisulu comments: 'All I wanted was to see how the children were doing and maybe donate a few books. I was taken aback when the headmaster told me that I must seek clearance from the regional director. Surely, former students need to be treated with some respect.'

At a writers' workshop at the book fair later in the week, Sisulu was less accommodating. A second article in *The Herald* (also 5 August) cites Sisulu's remarks at the workshop. The article begins, 'Governments within the Southern Africa Development Community should ensure that more books published by local authors are integrated into the school curriculum instead of imported books by foreign authors' ('Include Books in Syllabus'). Sisulu is quoted as saying that Shakespeare's popularity with African readers is due to his presence in the school curriculum and that if African writers are also included, their popularity will also be assured. Citing examples from other areas of the world where books have been promoted in churches and even at athletic events, Sisulu also proposed that 'stakeholders in the book industry must also formulate aggressive ways of marketing books instead of traditional marketing systems'. One wonders if publishers ever pay much attention to the suggestions of their writers.

Yvonne Vera (Zimbabwe)

In recent years, few writers from sub-Saharan Africa have had such success and acclaim heaped upon them as Yvonne Vera, almost since the publication of her first book, a collection of short stories, *Why Don't You Carve Other Animals* (1992). The volume was published in Canada where Vera began writing as a student. Her first novel, *Nehanda* (1993), was also written in Canada but co-published with Baobab Books, in Zimbabwe, thus beginning one of the most fruitful relationships between any African writer and her (or his) publisher. Without that nurturing relationship between Yvonne Vera and her editor, Irene Staunton, it is unlikely that Vera's career would have moved so quickly into a high gear or received such international acclaim. I am unaware of any other relationship between a writer and an editor at a publishing house on the continent that has been quite so productive and beneficial to both parties.

Vera was born in Bulawayo, one of the largest cities in Zimbabwe (then Rhodesia), in 1964. Her mother was a school-teacher, her father equally accomplished. A love of books was established before she began attending primary school (she could read and write before her formal education began); more importantly, she began writing when she was still a child. She remembers leaving notes and poems she had written for her mother when her mother was ill. In school, other students identified her as 'the writer'. After graduation from secondary school, she had the benefit of a vacation in Europe. The galleries in Florence and Venice particularly engaged her. Subsequent trips to the United States (New York) and Canada culminated in her matriculation at York University, Toronto, where she studied Fine Arts with an emphasis on film. Her education was clearly cosmopolitan. She stayed at York long enough to earn three degrees, the final one a PhD in literature.

Vera's third book, *Without a Name* (1994), was the first one she wrote in Zimbabwe, while at home on a holiday. Set against the backdrop of her country's civil war (itself a controversial topic), *Without a Name* was the first of her books to take a darker turn, shattering convention by focusing on the rape of a young woman who leaves the country for the city. The novel (and the two earlier books) was short-listed for the Commonwealth Writers' Prize for the African area, an award Vera won two years later for her third novel, *Under the Tongue* (1996). Neely Tucker (in a review in *Worldview*) has described that novel's focus as 'Incestuous rape, spousal murder, the death of a young child; it's not a happy place'. As in the previous novel, the country's recent struggle for independence plays a significant part in the shattered psyches of the main characters. Besides winning her country's major literary award – the Zimbabwe Book Publishers Association Literary Award – the following year, Vera was awarded the Swedish Voice of Africa Literary Award for *Under the Tongue* in February 1999, which included a monetary prize of SEK 100,000 ($12,600).

By the time Vera had won the prestigious Swedish award, she had already published her fourth and in many ways her most accomplished novel, *Butterfly Burning* (1998). Her dense and elliptical narrative, confusing to some of her readers, once again tackles a daring topic, better left unmentioned (or under the tongue, to use one of the author's own metaphors) in Zimbabwean society: abortion. As is true of her earlier works, in this one there is brutality and pain inflicted on women as well as on men, though the setting is not contemporary but loops back to the 1940s, to a ghetto of Bulawayo during the colonial era when Africans were often treated as if they were living in a penal colony. With this novel and the two earlier ones, which form a kind of unconventional trilogy, Vera also emerged as a strong feminist writer, at odds with the masculine hegemony of her country. Affinities between Vera's novels and Toni Morrison's are increasingly apparent.

When I asked Vera specifically about her controversial subject matter – rape, incest, abortion – she responded by saying:

> To the extent that women still experience the highest degree of social pressure and stigmatization in Zimbabwe, and that these various aberrations of human contact affect them the most, my writing is a critique of the weaknesses in my society. The position of women needs to be reexamined with greater determination and a forceful idea for change. In Zimbabwe, as perhaps elsewhere in the world, there is limited understanding of each moment of a woman's worst tragedy or her personal journey. Women have been expected to be the custodians of our society as well as its worst victims, carrying on, no matter how hemmed in they feel and how abandoned in their need. There are beauties, too, and I write about them, our combined capacity as Zimbabwean men and women to endure all we have experienced in colonial times and today. I hope my novels bring out our best capacities and characteristics. (e-mail to author, 23 January 1999)

Does Vera consider herself a feminist writer? What, in fact, does it mean to be a feminist in Zimbabwe at the end of the twentieth century?

> I know feminism is such a contested term and I am not sure what it means when I answer yes! But I certainly am involved and passionate about women's issues, and write about women as you describe. In Zimbabwe there is great suspicion and superstition about feminism. There is fear; after all, the resources over which we fight, especially regarding property, are limited. Yet it is about more than this – it is

about our entire grounding as human beings seeking equal attention in all areas of our existence. It is vital for women to seek this resolution through their different voices. There is no obstructing resentment toward women writers in Zimbabwe, there is celebration. Perhaps women came much later to the field, and added to the variety of our country's literature.

In an earlier response to my questionnaire, Vera was pleased to note that from among her own people she has received more letters and questions from men than from women.

No other writer of the current generation can duplicate Yvonne Vera's literary success, though Ben Okri (of the previous generation) comes closest to Vera because of an equally impressive string of literary awards. The difference between the two, however, is that Vera decided to leave Canada, where no doubt she could have found her niche in a comfortable, if not lucrative, academic position, and return home – home being in this case both Bulawayo and Zimbabwe. After her earlier books had appeared in Canadian editions, Vera felt that her reading audience was not where it should be. 'I needed to come back home,' she told Ish Mafundikwa during an interview for *Skyhost* in 1997. 'I did not want to be interpreted but to be heard. I find that immediacy very vital.' Asked directly about her decision to return to Bulawayo, Vera responded lyrically:

I was born and raised in Bulawayo. It is the second city, so to speak, in Zimbabwe. Each of the inhabitants here feels a certain marginal identity, and therefore an irrational and fierce love for being here. Bulawayo people have always shaped their identities around the notion of being peripheral, of being drought-stricken for example, and at different times, of political secondariness. The landscape is very distinct, flat for distances, and the thorn bushes scattered everywhere in their sparse vegetation, blooming when they can. And anthills. The sky so low you could lick it. Very blue in winter. In all my time in Canada, I never lost its heartbeat, and I was never complete. I felt I was in transit, even more marginal there, than I could ever be, though Canada is lovely and peaceful. It is almost true that I could never find my vocation without my residence there. Finally, I had to be me, no longer in transit under another sky. I have always loved Bulawayo in a complete manner. The weather is beautiful all year, very high temperatures in October, but good weather. I missed my home and knew that I had to return. Perhaps none of it would work and I would have to set off again, to some other land. I have never wanted to be a writer in exile – I hope never to have to make a decision to leave Zimbabwe, for whatever reason. I hope to continue in this small town, with its gentle and unhurried pace. (e-mail to author, 23 January 1999)

In 1998, she was appointed director of the National Gallery in Bulawayo, a full-time position. Her work keeps her in touch with other artists. These duties, specifically, are designed

to ensure the smooth running and function of the National Gallery in Bulawayo in its role to exhibit the best of our visual art products across the various media. To facilitate artists, and promote the growth of art and artists in the region, where possible to offer training and education. I am tasked with the role to preserve works of art in the region and build an archive of representative works. Often, we offer ourselves as a center for cultural activity and hold events not only in visual art but in performance art, and offer a lecture series, and host book fairs. To our visitors, to generate among them an appreciation of our art and our gallery space.

What does it mean to be a bestselling author in Zimbabwe? To answer that question, we must turn to Yvonne Vera's editor at Baobab Books, Irene Staunton. When I asked her what would be a successful book in terms of sales in Zimbabwe, she replied, eight or maybe nine hundred copies. No author is going to get rich, in spite of the occasional sales of foreign rights. Besides the Canadian editions, the American publisher Farrar, Straus & Giroux began publishing Vera's novels in 2000. There have been translations of several titles, though in most cases these only bring in a few hundred dollars, which must be split fifty–fifty with Baobab Books.

So how does Yvonne Vera see herself as a writer, even though in terms of age she is still at an early stage of her literary career? She has been able to avoid many of the problems faced by other African writers of her generation, was privileged to have a sympathetic and nurturing editor at Baobab Books, and was fortunate to be able to devote time to her craft in spite of her full-time duties at the National Gallery of Bulawayo. 'The task of the writer is simply to write, to tell the story convincingly, to create a world, and write with an eloquence and artistry that announces the work as originally conceived and superbly executed. This is the challenge and the measure which every writer turns to' (e-mail to author, 30 September 1998). As she told Ish Mafundikwa: 'I have no choice, I have to write in order to share, in order to liberate my imagination … What I have to worry about is where do I grow from here, how do I grow.'

The careers of these five writers are widely varied, yet they also share a number of important similarities. The youngest of the group, Yvonne Vera (born in 1964), has been the most successful in receiving continuous support from her publisher and the literary community. She has not had to divert as much of her energy into seeking out the next publisher for her books as has, for example, Véronique Tadjo. Though her readership has been somewhat restricted to Zimbabwe or the continent itself, Vera has the good fortune of a small coterie of readers who actively welcome her works as they are published. She has, in fact, been able to write for her own people, which is no doubt every African writer's dream. True, some of her African readers have found her novels difficult, but Vera nevertheless appears to have established a comfortable relationship with those readers and with the literary world itself.

Vera shares with the others a cosmopolitan, international education, including advanced degrees, which is true of a significant number of African writers since the *négritude* poets began writing in the early 1930s. Only Tutuola, discussed in Chapter 1, had a notably different education than the writers examined here, though Chinua Achebe's education was entirely within his country's boundaries. Tadjo was born in Paris; Vera began writing while she was a student in Canada; Sisulu began her professional writing in Europe; Ekwensi continued his education in London. Cordor might never have left his country of birth and pursued further education in the United States if Liberia had been politically stable.

Cordor is also the writer who has encountered the most difficulty in achieving success with his writing. For better or for worse, British and French colonialism – particularly the high standards of their education systems – were more likely to produce a climate in which an African would begin writing than has been the case in Liberia which has no colonial legacy. What did the United States care about Liberia? Since education was important in the British and French colonies – if nothing else it produced the necessary bodies for an indigenous civil service – local publishing houses were eventually established in these areas, albeit mostly for the textbook market. Véronique Tadjo's publishing record may be akin to balancing on a high wire, yet she appears to have achieved her goal of publishing books simultaneously in France and the Ivory Coast, something that can be said of few other writers on the continent.

Tadjo's concern about the availability of her works for African readers, of being *read* by her people, approaches a level of urgency articulated by the continent's writers in the last decade. Much of Cordor's angst in the years of his exile, it can be speculated, is the result of one stark reality: cut off from his people, he cannot be read by them. Elinor Sisulu expresses a more optimistic version of this urgency by stressing the need for imaginative literature for African children, especially when this writing is rooted in the historical, given the diminished emphasis on storytelling in many African societies. Vera not only returned to her roots physically, but began writing about the place of her birth, Bulawayo, only after she had written several earlier works. Ekwensi's fame has been worldwide, but his royalties have tapered off to almost nothing, perhaps because (as he says) he decided to remain in his motherland.

This need for connectedness with the culture and with one's own people appears as a kind of leitmotif, both in the authors' responses to my questionnaire and in innumerable other places where writers speak out about their work. Remembering the earliest years of his writing, Gilbert Doho, a Cameroonian novelist and dramatist who writes in French, describes his years at a bilingual grammar school in the Bay of Victoria. The student's 'journey' was supposed to be spiritual, but it was at school that Doho first became interested in becoming a writer because all the writers he was exposed to in his classes were European.

> Since then, I have always written with the objective to root everything in Cameroon. I dreamed of printing houses where local literary production could be carried out for the easy transportation from

Cameroon to other [areas]. I wanted to be published but primarily in Cameroon. I wanted others to come over here and fetch our products. It was probably this nationalistic conception of books that contributed to and still remains my crusade as a writer. I think that if there is pride in being read, this is doubled when materials are rooted in our soil. Fame from outside has a sour taste. (letter to author, 15 July 1997)

Doho is enough of a nationalist to worry about how there can ever be a true literature for his country if the writers rely on publishers and editors in France. Thus, he sees the need for his countrymen to fight not only for the integrity of a given novel or drama, i.e. its content, but also for the manner in which the work is produced. He believes that famous Cameroonian writers such as Mongo Beti, Ferdinand Oyono and more recently Calixte Beyala have done more harm than good to Cameroonian writing. Ironically, Doho notes, if they had not been published overseas, they might never have been known at all. But, still: 'The deliberate choice to be published from without has stopped the development of publishing within Cameroon and thus contributed to the growth of the "invisible writer." There are thousands in Cameroon who have written, but are nowhere to be seen.'

After being humiliated by both French and Cameroonian publishers – including having a volume of poems accepted by a French publishing house and subsequently rejected without explanation – Doho concluded that the only solution was to establish a literary co-op, a

thrift and loan association where ten writers come together, contribute £50 each, which amounts to £500 monthly. After having read, given constructive criticism to the monthly chosen writer among the group, his manuscript, typed and set, is handed over to an editor for the printing of copies. This enables the group and the writer to have a book with an ISBN number and the possibility of being distributed both locally and internationally. This is how we could survive [as writers] in a context of repression where books and docile intellectuals control the market.

Yet, once again, economic reality has destroyed a well-intentioned plan. University salaries in Cameroon have been so reduced by inflation that few academics, who are better paid than people in many other fields, could afford to contribute to the co-op. Doho concludes that a writer would have to starve himself to see his work in print. So much for good intentions.

Doho and many other African writers have found themselves trapped within a vicious circle. If they publish overseas, editors with no understanding of their culture may try to influence what they are saying (let alone the way they say it), and their books may not be read by their own people. Yet publishing on the continent has its own pitfalls (limited editorial guidance, inferior production and restricted distribution). Is it better to be published overseas and at least be known outside one's country, or to be published within and possibly remain unread except by a wealthy elite? How can a writer cater to two distinctly different audiences?

In spite of what some of my creative writing students have told me ('I write for myself'), I believe that writers write to be read. I also believe that most writers want to be (or at least expect to be) read by their own people, who are usually the people about whom they write. Those writers whose careers have been discussed in this chapter assert that art is always rooted in the writer's specific culture, time and place in spite of what we often regard as a timeless universality. Years ago, Virginia Woolf wrote about her dilemma in a slightly different context, as breaking away from tradition and writing something new and different – modern. In 'Modern Fiction' Woolf wrote:

> so that, if a writer were a free man and not a slave, if he could write what he chose, not what he must, if he could base his work upon his own feeling and not upon convention, there would be no plot, no comedy, no tragedy, no love interest or catastrophe in the accepted style, and perhaps not a single button sewn on as the Bond Street tailors would have it. (p. 106)

In their convictions, their goals and aspirations, African writers are no different from other writers around the world.

- 'I love language and form.' (Yvonne Vera, e-mail to author, 3 October 1998)
- 'I write because I wish to prove to *others* that I can do it as well as anybody else.' (Nuruddin Farah, 'Why I Write' 1988)
- 'My goal as a writer is such that when I die, I will want to be remembered.' (Jekwu Ikeme, letter to author, 12 August 1997)

- 'My goal as a writer is to educate, entertain, and move mankind the world over.' (Kehbuma Langmia, letter to author, 26 June 1997)
- 'As a writer, I would like to share my love of life with my readers … I would like to explore the mind, see how far it can expand in terms of imagination. I would like people to enjoy what I write, but not to believe I think all life is one, long happy ride: it can be hell, a living hell. I would like them to accept that, along with the love and kisses. I would like our governments in Africa to let us explore the limits of our imagination.' (William Saidi, letter to author, 24 April 1997)
- 'My goal as a writer is to help diminish the bad and actively promote the good.' (F. Odum Balogum, letter to author, 12 August 1997)
- 'My goal as a writer: first and foremost to communicate an idea or feeling I have and which I believe may interest others.' (Jare Ajayi, letter to author, October 1997)
- 'For me the excitement of writing was to transform, enlarge, enrich and transfuse language.' (Lenrie Peters, letter to author, 24 October 1997)
- 'I believe in poetry as talking words, as possessed words, as words that must find an object to move, as words purged of the impunity of excess … To me, poetry can tap deep into the resources of history – it can reactivate dormant images, and give the past a life in the present, and allow us to go back to the school of the dead and revisit their restless skeletons and learn from their muted voices.' (Tijan M. Sallah, *Network 2000*, 1997)

Almost since they began publishing, African writers have rooted their works deeply within their specific cultures. In *Things Fall Apart*, Chinua Achebe may have parenthetically explained more of his people's cultural expressions and practices than he would have if he had been free to write what he wanted, but these glosses on traditional Ibo culture meant that his book was readily understood *both* by his own people *and* by those outside his own tribe, country and continent. Educating his Ibo readers about their rapidly changing world was no less important than educating his other readers about a specific Nigerian culture that was losing its traditions more quickly than it was acquiring new ones. Amos Tutuola, unhampered by academic concepts about what a novel is and what it can do (and therefore, perhaps, freer than many others to write what he wanted), plunged boldly into the western literary market and let it do with him what it would. The *négritude* poet, Léopold Sedar Senghor, in one of his most famous poems, 'Prayer to Masks', envisions a new relationship between Africa and the West, in which the former is no longer on the receiving end but provides 'the leaven that the white flour needs'. Nevertheless, he proclaims that Africans are still connected to their immediate environment: 'They call us cotton heads, and coffee men, and oily men, / They call us men of death. / But we are the men of the dance whose feet only gain power when they beat the hard soil' (Moore and Beier [eds], *The Penguin Book of Modern African Poetry*, p. 233).

The list of examples could be extended almost indefinitely, but two more – from writers still in the early stages of their careers – will suffice. Jekwu Ikeme, a Nigerian poet who has had more than his share of 'repeated failures at getting my voice heard, my work read and my dreams lived' (letter to author, 12 August 1997), nevertheless articulated the almost ubiquitous feelings of his compatriots across the continent, plus a dogged optimism that he will still succeed:

> As a writer, I write to inform, to educate, to share my views and thus contribute to the process of re-definition and re-discovery of ourselves as human beings. My art is geared towards celebrating and asserting my cultural heritage. Through my works, I affirm the human claim to dignity, and justice, the good life and happiness. I am one of those that strongly believe that writers have a responsibility to their society; as the visionary, the teacher, the conscience of the society, he defines the mission and gives focus to the march through life and therein lies the sublimer dimension of art.

Or, in the words of Segun Durowaiye, a Nigerian writer who has published short stories in local newspapers: 'For in a world where there is no money to buy the good things of life – a world where poverty reigns supreme like in Africa, the educated few and not-so-educated need creative stories to make them happy in times of depression. They need something to console them. To ginger them up' (letter to author, 26 August 1997).

CHAPTER 4

. . . .

African Publishers, African Publishing

[A] major problem of independent African publishers is the quality of books we publish. Even though it is improving, it is still not satisfactory … little thought is given to the need to design attractive covers … editing, proof-reading, indexing are often done perfunctorily; the printer with the lowest quote is selected even when his work is demonstrably poor, in the name of saving, and the equally bad economics of large print runs ostensibly to lower the unit costs are practiced with disastrous results. (Walter Bgoya, quoted in Zell, 'The Production and Marketing of African Books', *Logos*, 1998)

Textbooks … will reveal glaring spelling errors and bad grammar even in the preliminary pages and the blurb. The paper, the design, layout and illustrations are sub-standard. The printing and binding are awful, displaying bad imposition on the printer's part, so that printed lines on the opposite sides of corresponding pages do not 'merge.' There will be 'see through' because the lines were not properly 'backed-up.' Uneven inking and bad registration turn print into smudge. (Henry Chakava, quoted in Zell, op. cit.)

§ ENTERING a bookshop in many areas of the African continent may not be an enticing moment. Most are drab and uninviting, consisting of one poorly lit room. The majority of the books on the shelves are government-approved texts for specific courses from primary schools through to the end of secondary school. In recent years the majority of these books have been printed in Africa; typically they have two-colour covers, with more space given to bold print than appropriate illustrations. Other books almost always in stock are religious tracts of one kind or another (since so many schools in Africa were started by missionaries) and a wide selection of Bibles. There is usually a small selection of self-help titles, mostly related to business. The stock almost always includes books that are shelf-worn, with faded and curled-up covers, suggesting that sales are sluggish. A considerable proportion of the available space is devoted to stationery for schools and small businesses, and perhaps a few art supplies. Another section typically stocks newspapers and local periodicals, with an occasional publication (*Time*, *The Economist*, glossy international women's magazines and movie magazines), often several weeks out of date.

In the large cities, the bookshops are usually more inviting. They may contain a section (or at least a shelf or two) devoted to African writers, with both locally published titles and those from abroad, such as the Heinemann African Writers Series. More prominently displayed, though, will be a selection of recent European and American bestsellers – both paperback and hardback books, fiction and non-fiction as well as a smattering of expensive imported children's titles – especially by writers whose works have sold well in the West: Harold Robbins, Jacqueline Susann, Irving Wallace and, more recently, Stephen King. These are books that only the well-to-do can afford. I can't help remembering an image of an African reader embedded in my mind from a momentary glimpse in an airport terminal: a woman in purdah, with only her eyes showing, but carrying nestled in her arm a hardbacked copy of Jackie Collins's *Thrill*. Sadly, American schlock fiction is everywhere around the world. Along with pornography, the United States sets the standard. Why shouldn't Africans read the same junk that Americans read?

The Zimbabwe International Book Fair

No wonder that the Zimbabwe International Book Fair has been such a success in recent years. With stores throughout the African continent in need of major innovations, with publishers and writers eager to change their lot, there is plenty of room for improvement. One hopes the almost infectious atmosphere of the now annual ZIBF will continue to have a major impact on every aspect of African publishing. Held outside in the sculpture garden behind the National Gallery in Harare, the ZIBF throbs with excitement. Street musicians as well as their more professionally trained counterparts perform daily in adjacent areas; children dressed in colourful school uniforms weave in and out of the crowds and often participate in the major events of the fair (painting, weaving, drawing, for example, as well as the more obvious 'literary' presentations of plays and skits). The tents put up to house the displays of the participating publishers and international agencies are scattered among the beautiful trees and permanent fixtures of the sculpture gardens, which include a larger-than-life metal rhinoceros. At the gate outside the gardens, crowds line up for entry, winding among the hawkers of food and merchandise that one encounters in almost any African city. Here, however, these street vendors seem part and parcel of the entire tenor of the fair itself: pleasure for the mind as well as the senses.

The first ZIBF was held in 1983, three years after Zimbabwe's independence. It was a modest event in its early years: one of the early fairs, for example, was held inside Kingston's Bookshop in the centre of Harare. Since 1989 the fair has been an annual event (held during the first week in August), preceded by a two-day Indaba, or what might be called a scholarly conference, which focuses on the annual theme of the fair. In recent years, these themes have included 'Reading is Development', 'Science and Technology', 'Freedom of Expression and the Press', 'National Book Policy', 'Children', 'Books for Business' and 'Libraries'. During the most recent year for which there are figures (1998), '300 direct exhibitors took part in ZIBF 98 representing 500 publishers … from 50 countries. 19,645 visitors attended, including 9240 trade and professional visitors during the traders' days and 10,405 members of the public on the public days' ('*Facts and Figures from ZIBF 98: Children*').

From its modest beginnings, the fair – under the thoughtful guidance of Trish Mbanga and Margaret Ling – has mushroomed into a major international event for book publishers from around the world. Initially under the management of the Ministry of Information, Posts and Telecommunications, since 1990 the event has been controlled by the Zimbabwe International Book Fair Trust, an independent body. Clearly, without international donor support (mostly but not exclusively from Europe) there would be no fair as it is recognized today, but European and American publishers and international organizations do not dominate proceedings. In 1998, for example, of the countries represented by exhibitors and visitors, thirty-two were from the African continent; the remaining twenty-six included Cuba, Jamaica, India, Indonesia, the Philippines and Vietnam. The intentions of some

American publishers whose booths contain tables overflowing with books seem questionable to me: are they trying to dump unsellable titles on the African continent? Nevertheless, it is impossible to consider the ZIBF as anything other than an African event.

For creative writers, the Book Fair is a boon, not simply because writers who might not otherwise have an occasion to meet each other have that opportunity ('writers need writers'); but also because 'satellite events', as they are referred to, focus on the writer/artist and virtually every aspect of his (or her) career. Thus, besides workshops for writers, there have been readings by writers at some of the city's important bookshops and literary hangouts; award ceremonies for creative writers (both the Noma Award and the Zimbabwe Book Publishers Association Annual Literary Awards); workshops on editing, book reviewing and peer critiquing; meetings of related interested parties (the Bellagio Publishers Donors Network and the African Publishers Network [APNET]); an annual African periodicals exhibit; and, of course, the Indaba itself which brings writers together with related interested parties (not just publishers and booksellers, but librarians, academics and government officials). In their overview of the ZIBF published several years ago, 'An Aspiring Frankfurt Emerges in Africa' (*Logos*, 1993), Trish Mbanga and Margaret Ling include an anecdote about Robert Mugabe:

> ZIBF91 nevertheless marked the beginning of the end of a protracted battle to convince the Zimbabwe government that its best interests lay in removing import duties and heavy sales tax on books. Local and visiting exhibitors alike were delighted when the country's President, Robert Mugabe, donned a 'Don't Tax Books' lapel badge as he toured the Fair and subsequently referred to 'stupid taxes' in his presentation. (p. 212)

There has also been negative publicity, often distorted by the western press. In both 1995 and 1996, the local gay community in Harare was prevented from having a booth at the fair – not by the Book Trust, but by the Mugabe government. In fact, the group should probably have been denied a booth by the Trust itself, since they had no publications to display. The Trust makes clear its belief in freedom of speech, though at times the Mugabe government has clearly moved in a counter direction.

At the American Library Association's annual conference in 1998, Margaret Ling explained what the fair has come to represent:

> The ZIBF is part of Africa's response to the globalisation of publishing and information dissemination, and to the globalisation of knowledge production itself. Drawing on the language of Southern Africa's freedom movement, one might describe the ZIBF as a cultural weapon in the war against Africa's marginalisation and exclusion. Whatever words are used, the important thing is that the ZIBF is made in Africa, is located decisively in Africa, is organised on African themes and has an African agenda ... We are committed to supporting the development of book reading, a book using and a book buying culture in Africa. We seek to be simultaneously a trade fair, a cultural celebration at the cutting edge of book-related policy development in Africa. (Ling, 'Response to Speakers', 1998)

No easy task, to be certain, but admirably stated.

Yet all is not well, despite the enthusiasm of both organizers and participants at the ZIBF. Hans M. Zell, one of the most respected observers of (and a direct participant in) the continent's publishing scene, has repeatedly noted during the last decade that publishing in Africa has reached crisis point. In spite of three hundred 'active indigenous firms with fairly sizable publishing programs, plus several hundred small imprints' (*Encyclopedia of Africa*, p. 537), there is a 'grave book famine in Africa' ('Africa – the Neglected Continent', *Logos*, 1990, p. 20), resulting in what Zell refers to as a 'bookless society'. He notes that it is not simply a matter of economics but 'corrupt regimes, capital flight, devastating years of drought and famine, political unrest, and the consequences of the major hikes in the price of oil' (p. 19). Moreover, as budgets for education have been drastically curtailed, 'funds for textbooks and library funds have dramatically declined'.

> [P]ublic libraries in Africa have been unable to purchase *any* new books over the past four or five years, much less to maintain their current periodical collections. Bookshops have empty shelves; schools are without books; research has been crippled; teachers and scholars are divorced from the materials needed to pursue their studies, to maintain their understanding of developments in their disciplines elsewhere in the world. (pp. 21–2)

Libraries, especially, have become totally dependent on donations from the West. Scholars in the West are certainly aware of the situation, since when they renew a personal subscription for a periodical they are asked to take out a second subscription for an African library. Zell notes a high 'mortality rate among new [African publishing] companies'. Relations between African writers and their publishers are often at breaking point. Zell quotes Onwuchekwa Jemie who, in the Nigerian *Guardian* (25 January 1987), 'lumped all publishers together as "mostly liars and cheats"' (p. 24). None of the earlier problems (language, cost of production and distribution, literacy and so on) has gone away; they have simply been exacerbated by additional ones.

Zell has had several decades of experience publishing on the continent and publishing African materials outside it. He was the director of the University of Ife Press in Nigeria and has held other positions on the continent. Besides editing and publishing African materials for many years, since 1975 he has edited the *African Book Publishing Record*, a quarterly book trade and bibliographic journal that has attempted to bring some kind of order to the vast disarray of publishing across the continent. Above all, he has worked for increased accountability in African publishing.

Yet for all his enthusiasm for the continent itself and for publishing, he is not afraid to describe things as they are instead of as they should be. Commenting on the state of some books published in Africa, describing them as 'atrociously produced', Zell has said:

> Too often the local books are poorly edited, badly designed, sloppily proofread, coupled with careless or slipshod printing and finishing, with the net result that the finished product, sadly, looks decidedly amateurish.
>
> I have seen African books recently – quite a few, but not all, from Nigeria – with pages not straight, some pages smudged with big blobs of ink, uneven density and print image, half-tones barely legible, poor finishing, binding, trimming (with sometimes even the crop marks still showing), creased paper and other serious flaws. There seems to be a lack of quality control throughout. ('The Production and Marketing of African Books', *Logos*, 1998, p. 107)

Examining such books, one might conclude that publishing in Africa has not progressed since the days of the Onitsha pamphlets.

Zell is equally disturbed by the marketing of their works by some African publishers. He questions why African publishers, who constantly complain about unfair competition from the West, do not avail themselves of the networks that have been set up to help them promote their books. Librarians have explained that they do not have adequate information about African publications, yet some of these publishers never bother to have their books included in the *African Book Publishing Record*, a free service (which Zell edits). Nor do they avail themselves of the services offered by the African Publishers Network (APNET). Additionally, any number of book trade listings in the West, that is free publicity, are typically ignored.

Zell's remarks are corroborated by any number of the more successful African publishers, including Walter Bgoya and Henry Chakava. Chakava, for example, has commented on the lack of professionalism among his peers:

> As far as I am aware, there is no African publisher who produces advance publicity on new and forthcoming titles. Few bother to print promotional leaflets, only a handful produce annual catalogues. Most catalogues have incomplete and outdated information. Blurbs could do with a little editorial intervention. The essential bibliographic information, such as ISBN, year of publication, price and marketing restrictions, etc, may be missing. (quoted in Zell, 'The Production and Marketing of African Books', p. 104)

Given these conditions, Zell indicates that he can understand why African writers are frustrated, though they shouldn't be obliged to accept a second-rate product simply because it is produced in Africa. Zell's frustration level has clearly been breached:

> All of this is old ground. It has been stated and restated, by me and others, on more occasions than I can remember. So, how many more donor-supported Indabas; how many more workshops; how many more training seminars; how many more conference recommendations and resolutions are needed before at least the majority of African publishers become more business-like and professional? Until they do, they don't deserve anyone's sympathy and shouldn't be in the business of publishing in the first place. They certainly have no grounds for

complaint if Msungu [White Man] competitors snatch business on their doorsteps. (p. 106)

A word or two about publishing in India might be germane here. The Indian sub-continent shares any number of obvious similarities with Africa south of the Sahara. Illiteracy is high, there are multiple languages (including thirteen official ones for all government documents), poverty and economic stagnation are as ubiquitous as they have been in Africa, yet book publishing is and has been thriving for decades. Yes, books in India are typically produced on the cheapest of paper, often newsprint, yet the other troublesome aspects of book production have been overcome. Books have not become 'luxury items' as they are in Africa but are affordable for school-children and adults. Indian national book policy has supported an inexpensive production and distribution system for years. In 1996, an Indian child with the equivalent of one American dollar could purchase seven books. Much has been done by the government to make books and reading central to people's lives. Indian book publishers who attend the Zimbabwe International Book Fair are often dismayed when they examine the books produced by their African counterparts.

It is not as if publishing in Africa is so recent that one can expect only the results of inexperience. On the contrary, publishing in Africa has an illustrious tradition going back several centuries to the 'advent of Islam ... [B]y the seventeenth century various Arabic scripts were in circulation in the main urban and trading centers of the western Sudan' (*Encyclopedia of Africa*, p. 536). With colonialism and the arrival of Christianity, publishing became mission-directed, with texts designed to support the goals of missionary education as well as the production of Bibles in indigenous languages. Around the middle of the eighteenth century, the 'first mission printing press was established' in Nigeria; in South Africa, the first mission press (Lovedale in the Eastern Cape) started publishing in 1861; in Kenya, the first was set up in 1887. The Onitsha publishers began producing their books fifty years ago. It is not exactly as if facilities are lacking across the continent for the production of quality books and pamphlets.

Publishing in Kenya

Detailed information about publishing in specific African countries is difficult to obtain, but two recent books about Kenya provide a more comprehensive overview than is available for most other areas: *Publishing in Africa: One Man's Perspective* (1996) by Henry Chakava, and *Publishing and Book Trade in Kenya* (1997) by Ruth L. Makotsi and Lily K. Nyariki. Chakava's perspective is broader than that of his colleagues and particularly revealing because the obstacles he identifies exist across the continent. For example, he cites the number of languages on the African continent (1200), a figure that can be found elsewhere, but then explains that since only half of them have been transcribed, 'This means that many Africans do not have access to materials written in their own languages' (p. 73). Even English and French, two of the most widely used languages on the continent, 'cannot be read by more than twenty-five percent of the population in the countries where they are used' (p. 97). Although the continent's book output 'doubled from 4300 titles in 1965 to 8700 titles in 1978' (p. 96), Africa – according to UNESCO – contributes only 1.2 per cent of the total of the world's book production (p. 81). Chakava states that approximately 65 per cent of the continent is illiterate (others say 50 per cent) but, perhaps more meaningful, 'The publisher in Africa publishes for only about twenty percent of the population' (p. 73). Chakava does not indicate how many people within that 20 per cent actually purchase books.

The authors of both of these books provide a reasonably unblemished overview of publishing in Kenya, beginning with a statement by Makotsi and Nyariki that 'The Kenya publishing scene has for a long time been riddled with problems' (p. 1), yet 'Kenya has performed better in publishing development than most other African countries' (p. 65). The authors admit that publishing in Kenya has often developed out of a response to external publishing, implying that this is no way to nurture a publishing industry. They admit, also, that only textbook publishing is economically safe, and likely to provide adequate return on capital.

At the time when Makotsi and Nyariki published their study (1997), the population of Kenya was twenty-six million. There were sixteen 'full-fledged libraries' (p. 54) in the country, 600 bookshops and five major book distributors, but no distributor who reached 'all parts of the country' (p. 31). Textbook publishing accounted for 60 per cent of the total (p. 31), while the publishing industry employed approximately 500 people (p. 32), certainly a modest enough figure.

Regarding book production itself, Makotsi and Nyariki note that in Kenya paper is the single most expensive item in the production cost, amounting to about 60 per cent of the total, and 'yet there is a monopoly on paper production in Kenya with only one papermill in which the government has the majority interest' (p. 80). As is true of other countries, the paper imported for book production is highly taxed, as are printing inks, but, ironically, it is less expensive than locally produced paper (p. 105). It is easy to understand why so many books produced in Africa are printed on the cheapest paper available and why illustrations, if they exist at all, are entirely in black and white.

Successes in Kenyan publishing began with the East African Literature Bureau in 1947, an offshoot of the Ndia Kuu Press, originally set up by missionaries 'with offices in Dar es Salaam, Nairobi and Kampala, to produce educational and literary materials and to develop materials in local languages to cater for the needs of the growing literate population' (p. 25). It wasn't until almost twenty years later that the first truly indigenous publishing house was established: the East African Publishing House, in 1965. Somewhat later, the East African Community broke apart, yet publishing has continued to thrive in Nairobi. In 1986, Heinemann Educational Books (East Africa) evolved into East African Educational Publishers (managed by Henry Chakava). A number of smaller publishers, including some authors' self-publication ventures, were set up at the same time. Though publishing in indigenous languages has been attempted a number of times (most notably by Chakava), it is English that dominates the literary market in spite of the attempts of some of the area's major writers (Ngugi wa Thiong'o) to alter the scene. East African Educational Publishers, the largest, has a backlist of more than a thousand titles, most of them for the educational market. More importantly – at least for the creative writer – the house has been successful in bringing out local editions of many of the continent's significant writers (Chinua Achebe, Ayi Kwei Armah, Peter Abrahams, Alex la Guma, Elechi Amadi and Mariama Bâ, for example), by licensing many of these works from Heinemann (and the African Writers Series).

With a better communication infrastructure than most other countries – the transport system for distributing books is adequate, as is the postal system (compared to some countries where nothing of value is safe), and telephones work most of the time (Chakava, *Publishing in Africa*, p. 45) – publishing in Kenya ought to be a model for other countries. Yet Chakava is not particularly sanguine about his successes, which have been thwarted by innumerable obstacles, suggesting that it is diligence that has mattered more than anything else.

> Kenyan book publishers thus enjoy an exceptionally conducive environment by African standards. Yet, local private enterprise publishing has not flourished. About 40 percent of all publishing is done by the state. Imports from 20 percent and religious presses supply 10 percent. Most of the remaining 30 percent is in the hands of foreign-owned publishers. Since Kenya became independent in 1963, the indigenous publisher has been squeezed uneasily between his own government and the Kenyan branches of multinational companies. Emancipation is now in sight. It has been a long struggle. Why and how that struggle took place, and my own experience of it, illustrate the uncertain path of book development in the postcolonial world. Paved with good intentions, it is a path, in Kenya as in many other countries, subject to twists, turns, rocks, hard places, and pitfalls. (p. 45)

In his publishing, Chakava has also encountered some of the worst nightmares facing writers and publishers anywhere. When Ngugi wa Thiong'o made the decision to publish Gikuyu editions of his works, it was Chakava who agreed to become his publisher. The decision was not without repercussions; because Ngugi based some of his characters on real people, there were threats, direct and indirect, against both Chakava and his company, and the government removed Ngugi's books from official reading lists for schools. '[T]here have been other forms of censorship and harassment and the constant threat of litigation from members of the public who have felt libeled by Ngugi in his writings' (p. 61). Chakava says that he cannot speak for Ngugi or speculate about the ways in which the writer has suffered, including the fact that he has chosen to remain in exile. 'Had Ngugi continued to live in Kenya, write more books in this line [in

Gikuyu], and encourage his colleagues to support this venture, the program would have succeeded. In spite of my present setbacks in publishing in this area, I am waiting for the day when he will return home so that we can continue from where I stopped' (pp. 62–3).

The Kenyan example is representative of publishing in other African countries in one major way: if you want to make money in publishing, then concentrate on textbooks. Even in the film version of Chinua Achebe's *Things Fall Apart* (1972), which overlaps events from Okonkwo's era in Umuofia with more recent times in Ibadan, the film-makers couldn't resist making a dig at contemporary publishing. Okonkwo's grandson loses his job as a reporter on a major newspaper because he has attempted to expose a government minister whose crime is acquiring a monopoly on textbooks for school-children. The issue in the film is bribery, but the film-makers must have expected that viewers would be familiar with the high price of textbooks.

Although lucrative, textbook publishing is not without its own related limitations. Texts approved by a government ministry in one country will probably not be approved by the equivilant ministry in another. Thus sales are inevitably restricted to the producing country. Worse, to cite Chakava again, 'African publishers have little or nothing to offer in the facilitation of the free flow of knowledge between nations, one of the cardinal assumptions of international copyright. They are too poor and have little capacity and no experience in the buying and selling of rights' (p. 82). One wonders, in fact, how much actual selling of rights goes on at the Zimbabwe International Book Fair. How many textbooks get sold for reprint by publishing houses in other African countries?

Ditto creative works. How many novels published by a given African publisher are sold to a publisher in another African country, or for reprinting outside the continent itself? Chakava legitimately bemoans the practice of most celebrated African writers who chose to publish in Europe rather than in Africa. Though he has been able to sell the foreign rights to several of Ngugi's books that he first published in Gikuyu – most notably *Matigari* (1987) – Chakava does not own the rights to the earlier titles that have sold so widely around the world. At least inclusion in Heinemann's African Writers Series (and other series published by European publishers) guarantees some kind of distribution across the African continent – no doubt the reason why many writers are reluctant to publish their works locally. With internal distribution within a given African country often limited, there is almost no possibility of a novel or a volume of poems published in one country being successfully distributed in another. All one has to do is consider the time involved for a letter from one African country to reach an adjacent one, or attempt a telephone call from one country to another. Until the obstacles to distribution and communication are eliminated, publishing in Africa will continue to be a local affair.

The African Bestseller?

Gaining access to sales figures for creative works by African writers who publish on the continent is as difficult as the writers themselves having their works accepted by these publishers. African publishers were reluctant to respond to my questionnaire asking them what changes would be most beneficial in helping them become more successful. In my numerous direct interviews with publishers (and follow-up questions by e-mail and fax), when I questioned them about sales figures for specific titles, I noticed a hesitation in many of their responses as if they were uncertain whether these figures should be made public. I am aware that the concept of a bestselling book or author as we think of it in the West does not always have a natural equivalent in the global South, particularly in many areas of Africa. Yet African writers – in spite of the enormous obstacles they must overcome – continue to believe that it is possible to support themselves by writing.

As we have already noted, in once literary proud Nigeria the appearance of new creative works has been drastically curtailed. The country's most successful writers still publish new works outside their own country, though at least these same authors continue to be read and taught at home. The sales of *Things Fall Apart* have slipped considerably to a few hundred copies a year – largely, no doubt, due to the fact that Achebe's novel has not been part of the Nigerian senior secondary school syllabus. Declining book sales can also be directly related to the country's economic collapse during the years of military mismanagement. Answering my question about sales, Joop

Berkhout (the publisher of Spectrum Books) stated that Soyinka's books (*The Man Died* and *The Jero Plays*) sell two or three thousand copies a year in his editions (interview with author, 6 August 1998). The same is true of Cyprian Ekwensi's *Iska* and *Jagua Nana's Daughter*. Yet these are titles which once sold many thousands of copies annually. The greatest loss for the writer is the missed opportunity to develop literate and devoted readers. Many people who once read books for pleasure no longer do so.

There are certain exceptions, according to Berkhout – books that have better sales. *A Gift to the Troubled Land* (1991) by Segun Okunoren, a Yoruba writer, has seen annual sales increase to 10,000 copies since the novel became a set text for secondary schools. But even that figure, in a country of 120 million people, pales when compared with sales of books that became set texts for the School Certificate Examinations twenty years ago. Peter Enahoro's tongue-in-cheek *How to be a Nigerian* (1966) may be the best example of an on-going bestseller in the way that we regard such books in the West. According to Berkhout, it continues to sell several thousand copies each year.

The situation in Kenya (with a population less than a quarter of Nigeria's) for bestselling literary works is much more positive. Margaret A. Ogola's *The River and the Source* (1994) sold 120,000 copies in 1997, mostly because of its extensive use in secondary schools and Kenyan universities. A family saga with a focus on three generations of women, the novel has been reprinted a number of times and translated into at least one European language. Before the book became a set text in the schools, it sold five or six thousand copies per year. Ogola's publisher, Muthui Kiboi, the publishing manager of Focus Books, told me that the book has been supported by bulk sales to universities in the United States (interview with author, 6 August 1998). Asked about his second bestselling work, he mentioned *The Grapevine Stories* by Ngumi Kibera, which had sales of 4,300 copies midway through 1998. Kiboi was guardedly optimistic about the publishing of creative works. Both Ogola's and Kibera's works were awarded the Jomo Kenyatta Prize for Literature.

Outside set books for the educational market, the most successful Kenyan book in recent years has been John Kiriamiti's *My Life in Crime* (Spear Books, an imprint of East African Educational Publishers) which, since its original publication in 1984 – has sold 200,000 copies.

An excerpt from the back cover copy reads as follows:

> The late 1960s and early '70s may be remembered as the years of the great bank and other armed robberies in Kenya. This is the true story of one of the participants in some of those robberies, John Kiriamiti. In raw and candid language he tells the story of how he dropped out of secondary school when he was only fifteen years old, and for a time became a novice pickpocket, before graduating into crimes like car-breaking and ultimately into violent robbery. This spell-binding story takes the reader into the underworld of crime, and it depicts graphically the criminal's struggle for survival against the forces of law.
>
> John Kiriamiti who was imprisoned on 6 January 1971, after being convicted on a charge of committing robbery at Naivasha on 4 November 1970, left Naivasha Maximum Security Prison in August 1984, just five months after the publication of this fast-selling novel, which has now been reprinted.

Shades of Daniel Defoe's *Moll Flanders* and other rogue narratives. The seeming autobiography is described as a novel. According to Jeremy Ng'aug'a at Spear Books, the book is frequently reprinted in runs of 5000 copies, which are rapidly purchased by East African readers at a price the equivalent of about five American dollars (interview with author, 5 August 1998). In 1989, Kiriamiti published a second narrative called *My Life with a Criminal*. Both 'novels' are part of a series which East African Educational Publishers refer to in their promotion catalogue as 'Fast paced and educative! This series [Spear Books] is pitched to wholesomely entertain and educate young adults. Creativity is enhanced and life's challenges exposed. You will love it!' Chakava has remarked about the origin of the series: 'I noticed we were rejecting books about romance and crime for the Heinemann African Writers series. They were interesting but unsuitable for the classroom. They became our Spear Books. We opened up a new market, and other publishers followed … Surprisingly, although we started the series as an alternative to educational fiction, they are also quite widely read in schools' ('Talking Books', 1997, p. 15). The series has reached over forty titles since it was begun in 1975 and includes such works as *Life and Times of a Bank Robber* by John Kiggia Kimani; *Ben Kamba 009 in Operation DXT* by David Maillu; *A Prisoner's Letter* by Aubrey Kalitera; *Sugar Daddy's Lover* by Rosemary

Owino; and *Confessions of an AIDS Victim* by Carolyne Aballa. The popularity of pulp fiction knows no bounds.

According to Madieyna Ndiaye, directeur littéraire at Les Nouvelles Editions Africaines du Sénégal, in Dakar, the bestselling Francophone title in recent years is Mariama Bâ's *Une si longue lettre* (*So Long a Letter*), which is taught in many schools. As of May 1999, the combined sales for Bâ's novel were over 44,000 copies. Other bestselling titles – which like the Bâ title have sold well because of literary awards and/or school adoptions – include Bernard Nanga's *La trahison de Marianne* and Aminata Sow Fall's *La Grève des Bottu*. It is not clear if the sales figures of these books have been limited to Senegal or all of Francophone West Africa (letter to author, 19 May 1999).

B. D. Buma Kor, who distributes books in Cameroon under his own name Buma Kor & Co. Ltd, has recently begun publishing a Cameroon Writers Series, with titles aimed at Anglophone readers in the western part of the country. Print runs for the titles have been 3000 copies, 'but we hope that two of the titles will be adopted for use in schools next year [and] will enable us to print 10,000 copies each' (e-mail to author, 14 May 1999). Expectations for *Daughter of the Upstream Python*, a novel by Charles Alobwede D'Epie, are that sales will reach up to 30,000 copies. Buma Kor added that one of his students who recently studied the reading habits of the University of Yaoundé students concluded:

> most students read (even novels) to pass their examinations; some read fiction to pass the time or go to sleep; while most others take a book of fiction with them everywhere: whether they read it or not ... This looks like a general pattern in society at large. Hence, when we went into looking for literary material for the Cameroon Writers Series, we also drew this same conclusion and geared our editorial considerations to meet students' needs as well as the young working class. These are the ones who buy good fiction (with lots of romance or stories with traditional African plots).

African publishers clearly understand that sensation (romance, sex, crime, violence) appeals to African readers just as it does to readers elsewhere. Publishers of serious literature, however, realize that the only way that sales will be increased is by their works becoming approved for the classroom. B. Sodindwe Neube, an editor at the

Mambo Press in Harare, informed me that in order to gain access to the educational market, his press submits manuscripts before they are published to the Zimbabwean government and will, in fact, excise objectionable passages before publication in order to get a book approved (interview with author, 5 August 1998). Censorship of a manuscript before publication may sanitize it and result in additional sales but, in a wider context, it simply adds another layer of external control. One wonders what writers think of publishers willing to bend to such a process of government intervention.

In contrast to the situations in Nigeria, Kenya, Senegal, Cameroon and, to a lesser extent, Zimbabwe, one might surmise that the publishing of literary works by black writers in South Africa would be a more hopeful undertaking, but this has not been the case. The depressed economy rules, just as it does in so many other African countries. Books are luxury items. Colin McGee at Gondwana Books states that international bestselling authors may sell up to 50,000 copies of their books in paperback in South Africa. But most sell fewer than five thousand, and black African authors who sell in any quantity are 'few and far between' (e-mail to author, 29 September 1998). McGee says that there are 'No bookshops in traditional black residential areas' of the country. The determining factors are poverty and limited education. Nor, as we earlier noted, is there the possibility of developing African readers by introducing them to their own writers at local libraries since such libraries are non-existent.

Baobab Books

Still, serious publishers continue to attempt and sometimes succeed in developing literate reading audiences, as Baobab Books (in Zimbabwe) admirably demonstrated during ten years of publishing quality writing. The list of notable Zimbabwean writers published by Baobab Books includes Chenjerai Hove, Charles and David Mungoshi, Dambudzo Marechera, Alexander Kanengoni, Shimmer Chinodya and Yvonne Vera – an incredibly impressive list of writers to come from one country over such a short span of time and comparable to the flowering of Nigerian writers at the time of the country's independence forty years ago. Without Baobab Books, and without Irene Staunton as the publisher, the map of Southern African writing would look considerably different. The lesson to be learned from this? All it takes is the hard work of one publishing house, guided by integrity and quality, and the writers will appear. One wonders, for example, what might have happened to Tsitsi Dangarembga's literary career if her brilliant novel *Nervous Conditions* (1988) had been published by Baobab Books. It has never been a question of a lack of writers on the African continent; it has only been a lack of dedicated publishers.

Several of Baobab's writers (Chenjerai Hove, Shimmer Chinodya and Yvonne Vera) have received literary awards both from within the continent and outside it. Similarly, as we have seen with East African Educational Publishers, Baobab has published local editions of a number of the continent's most respected writers, including Nuruddin Farah, Chinua Achebe and Alex la Guma. Still, Baobab's focus has been on Zimbabwean authors, since the proximity to her writers permits Irene Staunton to do what editors rarely do these days: edit, demand that writers rewrite and then edit again, as long as necessary until the result is a quality work. Explaining her role as an editor, Staunton stated:

> I believe ... that the role of the publisher is not simply to publish books but to offer a supportive and critical interface through which writers can reflect upon their work before it is published; the publisher should not be afraid to discuss, challenge, ask, question the meaning of all the minutiae that make up the fiction. Words, phrases, sentences, metaphors, rhythms are the grasses out of which the characters, plots, and themes are woven and each one must be threaded and nuanced in the certainty that no other colour or texture will do.
>
> Once something has been written down, the ways in which it is perceived will vary, and the publisher must provide the final filter so that when the book appears, the author is as certain as he or she can be that what was written is what they wanted to communicate, what they wanted to say. This can be achieved through the exchange between the author and the editor/publisher but only if it is based on trust and mutual respect. (e-mail to author, 23 May 1999)

What is equally significant about Staunton's process is that it often results in works that demand close attention by their readers, in short, difficult texts. The best example is Yvonne Vera, whose novels often have a density comparable to those of Toni Morrison, who has at times been accused of obscurity by African American readers. To celebrate the tenth anniversary of the press, Baobab Books made the unprecedented move of simultaneously releasing three volumes of poetry: Chenjerai Hove's *Rainbows in the Dust*, Charles Mungoshi's *The Milkman Doesn't Only Deliver Milk*, and Chirikure Chirikure's *Hakurarwi* (the latter in a dual-language text in Shona and English). The three volumes are printed on quality glossy paper, sewn, and have colour-coordinated matching covers. The result is a publishing event unlike anything previously produced by an African publishing house.

And yet it has been anything but easy, concentrating on quality, instead of what would clearly be regarded as more readily marketable. Irene Staunton told me during an interview (4 August 1998) that most of the works published by Baobab have had to be subsidized, the route that she discovered to permit her to publish the books she accepts. Thus, she has to use her ingenuity and spend a great deal of time raising funds from international organizations and multinational corporations willing to support the publication of quality literature. This was also true of the three volumes of poetry released for the press's tenth anniversary. Publishing a single volume of poetry is anathema to most African publishers. Three at one time is unheard of.

In a few instances, Staunton has secured a co-publishing arrangement with another publisher abroad. Yet this can never be counted on – nor can subsidiary rights. Money from such rights, she says, dribbles in a little at a time and must be shared with the author fifty-fifty. Although she has licensed ten other editions of Chenjerai Hove's award-winning novel *Bones* (1988), the largest cheque she has ever received from another publisher for subsidiary rights was for $1000. The 50 per cent retained by the Press has never been enough to underwrite the expenses of another new title. Still, only quality books will command the respect of the literary world beyond the country's borders:

> In Africa being published well, i.e., ensuring that the book is properly copy-edited, proofed, given a well-designed cover and printed on relatively good paper is not always easily, lightly or cheaply achieved. This, however, is the only way that the publisher [can] ensure that an author from the third world is given critical attention in the first world. Authors should have the option of first being published, and

published well, in their own countries; and if the quality of the production reflects the quality of the work, then rights can be sold on into the first world rather than the reverse being true.

Typically, Baobab Books' titles are printed in editions of 2000 copies. The most successful sell eight or nine hundred copies a year, though Yvonne Vera's *Under the Tongue* sold 2000 copies in one year. Sales of five or six hundred copies in a given year constitute a bestseller. If she could count on significant library orders for the titles she publishes, that is orders from within Zimbabwe itself, Baobab's bottom line would be considerably improved. If she permitted passages in some of the books she publishes to be excised by the government censors, sales would also improve, but she has been admirably reluctant to do that. Her publications tend to win a majority of her country's literary awards, presented at the Zimbabwe International Book Fair each August. Yet in spite of all these awards and the acclaim by international organizations for Baobab Books, at the end of 1998, Academic Books (the press's parent company) suddenly announced that it was putting Baobab up for sale – presumably because of unfulfilled sales expectations. Months later, Irene Staunton's relationship with Baobab ended. Shortly before that change, in a comment that I asked her to make about her publishing philosophy, she wrote:

> Good publishers are like writers in several ways: they believe in books, they believe in the development of their list as a creation, as a statement, and as a coherent identity. They publish because they believe in what they are doing and want to give life to the voices that seem to them to have meaning and resonance in their own societies. They do so to enable these voices to be heard, and heard widely.

In spite of an unorthodox editor like Irene Staunton, it is not difficult to understand the level of scepticism that exists between so many African writers and their publishers. Each has differing expectations and perceptions of the realities of publishing. Too often for the writer, publication has resulted in no remuneration. Books are published and then badly distributed, yet when writers see them for sale, they assume that the publisher is getting rich. Genuine piracy of books is a problem in a number of African countries, but African writers at times believe that their own publishers are guilty of 'piracy', that is, providing deceptive information about sales figures. That belief was expressed by Olalare Oladitan at the ZIBF in 1998. On the other hand, publishers feel that writers have no idea of what is involved in book production. The report of the Arusha African Writers-Publishers Seminar in 1998 notes: 'There is a need for writers to understand the practical realities and costs involved in printing, warehousing, distribution and other processes. For their part, publishers need to consider what they can do to serve writers better' (p. 5).

At the seminar, the twenty participating writers and publishers from across the continent agreed on a new code of conduct to humanize and clarify the relationship between them. The document, 'A "New Deal" between African Writers and Publishers', sets out both publishers' expectations of their writers and writers' expectations of their publishers. There is nothing particularly original here, nothing beyond standard publishing expectations in the West, except both parties' admission that something needs to be done. Mostly, the agreement is an attempt to keep each party informed about what the other is doing, at all stages, beginning with the writer's submission of a manuscript right through to post-publication accountability for sales and royalties. Equally important are the concluding statements:

> The involvement of writers in discussions on all aspects of book issues in Africa should be encouraged and efforts to vitalise and support writers' associations. Likewise, we welcome and support the African Publishers Network mission statement, which reads: 'APNET's mission is to strengthen African publishers' associations through networking, training and trade promotion to fully meet Africa's need for quality books relevant to African social, political, economic and cultural reality.'
>
> There is a need to strengthen textbook production so that it can subsidise creative writing. There is also a need to encourage authors to write in indigenous African languages, to promote positive African values, and for publishers to find the means to publish such works and make them profitable and affordable in Africa.
>
> Strengthening African literature and culture through cooperation between writers and publishers should provide the guiding principle and aspiration for the two professions. (p. 35)

It is to be hoped that the Arusha conference will help to ease some of the on-going tensions between writers and their publishers.

. . . .

CHAPTER 5

'The Horror, the Horror'

We who write in Kenya, in Africa, in the Third World, are the modern Cassandras of the developing world, condemned to cry the truth against neo-colonialist and imperialist cultures and then be ready to pay for it with incarceration, exile and even death. (Ngugi wa Thiong'o, *Detained: A Writer's Prison Diary*, 1981)

What is the topic of literature? It began with the expulsion of Adam from paradise. What, in fact, writers do is to play around either with the myth of creation or with the myth of return. And in between, in parentheses, there is that promise, the promise of return. While awaiting the return, we tell stories, create literature, recite poetry, remember the past, and experience the present. Basically, we writers are telling the story of that return. (Nuruddin Farah, *Literature in Exile*, 1990)

§ THE end of the twentieth century has not been a particularly salutary time for many non-western writers, not simply those from Africa. The decade-long *fatwa* imposed on Salman Rushdie for the publication of *The Satanic Verses* (1988) stands out in many people's minds as emblematic of the times. Egyptian novelist Naguib Mahfouz was stabbed by a fanatical countryman who didn't much admire the Nobel Prize-winner's fiction. Bangladeshi writer Taslima Nasreen fled her country in the summer of 1994 for fear she would be murdered by some of her rabid readers (or, more likely, non-readers). These three writers survived what must certainly be too many Third World writers' worst nightmare: death. Not so Nigerian writer Ken Saro-Wiwa, whose hanging on 10 November 1995 by the Nigerian government revived the old stereotype of Africa as the dark continent.

African writers have suffered more indignities, threats, humiliations and genuine terror than their counterparts in the rest of the non-western world. One explanation for this disproportionate horror is no doubt due to what Ken Saro-Wiwa referred to as the African writer's need for engagement. Referring to his own situation as a spokesperson for the plight of the Ogoni people, Saro-Wiwa wrote: '[L]iterature in a critical situation such as Nigeria's cannot be divorced from politics. Indeed, literature must serve society by steeping itself in politics, by intervention, and writers must not merely write to amuse or to take a bemused, critical look at society. They must play an interventionist role ... the writer must be *l'homme engagé*: the intellectual man of action.' This quotation from *A Month and a Day: A Detention Diary* (1995: p. 81) was published shortly after Saro-Wiwa's execution, but he had already written numerous other non-fiction works, taking him away from his creative endeavours.

That move away from fiction, poetry and drama into the broad area of social commentary has been fraught with complications for many of the continent's writers, especially those from Nigeria. Creative work is a luxury that has eluded a number of the country's notable writers. In *The Trouble with Nigeria* (1983), Chinua Achebe launched a frontal attack on the problem, but dictators and military thugs are rarely known for their reading habits.

> The trouble with Nigeria is simply and squarely a failure of leadership. There is nothing basically wrong with the Nigerian character. There is nothing wrong with the Nigerian land or climate or water or air or anything else. The Nigerian problem is the unwillingness or inability of its leaders to rise to the responsibility, to the challenge of personal example which are the hallmarks of true leadership. (p. 1)

More than a decade later, Wole Soyinka's *The Open Sore of a Continent: A Personal Narrative of the Nigerian Crisis* (1996) extended the parameters of the discourse to a direct attack on Nigeria's so-called leader, the despised General Sani Abacha. Imagine William Faulkner or Ernest Hemingway – or more lately, someone like Anne Tyler – pulling themselves away from their fiction to tackle the daunting subject of leadership.

There are, of course, numerous western writers who have been as 'engaged' as Ken Saro-Wiwa. One thinks of Aldous Huxley, Arthur Koestler, Norman Mailer and Doris Lessing to name only a handful, but too many African writers have stopped writing or have had their careers abruptly ended because of a much wider web of censorship, of threats or genuine instances of imprisonment, or exile – the latter may be forced or voluntary, though it is sometimes impossible to distinguish between the two. The pages of *Index on Censorship* and the publications of PEN and Amnesty International are filled with examples of the systematic harassment of Africa's journalists, especially, but also of the continent's creative writers. There are simply too many troubling examples from Africa for any writer in the West (no matter how comfortable) to ignore, for what happens to a writer in Nigeria or Guinea or anywhere else involves all of us. But western writers who often expressed outrage at the treatment of their counterparts behind the Iron Curtain during the Cold War – have not always demonstrated particular concern about African or Third World writers. When the *fatwa* was placed on Salman Rushdie, there was an embarrassing silence from too many American writers and academics. The same applies to Ken Saro-Wiwa's death.

Still, the menacing environment in which African writers have written and continue to write ought to give writers in the West cause for concern. The problems have not gone away. Nor do they appear likely to in any immediate future. There are entire countries on the African continent where the creative writer has all but ceased to exist in any viable form – Sierra Leone, Liberia, Rawanda, the Congo, to mention only four – and too many others where literature is in a pathetic state of decline. The problems are not simply contemporary but go back as far as the beginning of post-colonial times.

Camara Laye: Death of the Artist

During the 1960s and 1970s, critics of African literature (myself included) often referred to Guinean writer Camara Laye as the author of the great African novel, *Le regard du roi* (1953), translated into English as *The Radiance of the King*. Almost equal praise had been heaped on *L'enfant noir* (1952), variously translated as *The African Child* or *The Dark Child*, Laye's autobiography (though referred to as a novel by some critics). The BBC, quoted on the dust-jacket, called Laye 'the first writer of genius to come out of Africa'. *L'enfant noir* was awarded the Prix Charles Veillon. Much of the early acclaim has been forgotten in recent years, no doubt because Laye died in 1980 when he was only fifty-two years old, by which time his productivity had been considerably reduced because of a series of unfortunate, if not tragic, events. There were also questions raised by Lilyan Kesteloot concerning the true authorship of *Le regard du roi*.

Laye was born in Kouroussa, in upper Guinea, in 1928, into a distinguished Malinké family. His father was a respected blacksmith and skilled artisan, whose work with gold Laye lovingly and mystically described in *L'enfant noir*. At nineteen, Laye left for France on a scholarship to study automotive mechanics and decided after completing the course that he wanted to stay on and earn a baccalaureate. Since his government scholarship had ended, he took odd jobs in order to support himself and pay for night-school. In his loneliness and apparent depression about his isolation from his motherland, he began writing down memories of his childhood. Those accounts of an almost idyllic childhood in the warmth of a loving family led to the publication of *L'enfant noir*, one of the purest and most honest accounts of childhood published anywhere, no doubt because it was written with little regard for publication.

Like Amos Tutuola, Camara Laye was another accidental writer, capping his first book with the publication of the much more ambitious work, *Le regard du roi*, a year later. Clarence, the main character of the novel, is a European of nondescript background whose presence in Africa is accidental. He has gambled away his meagre assets and seeks employment of the King, whom he believes will hire him simply because he is white, that is, superior to the Africans around him. Clarence's prejudices about Africans are, in fact, legion. Yet Laye renders the almost unfathomable possible by slowly eliminating the accretions of Clarence's myopic worldview and (by the end of the novel) transforming him into an African. *Le regard du roi* is one of those rare accounts of cultural syncretism, and is optimistic about our abilities as human beings to understand one another. Camara Laye was never given to the polemical or the rhetorical but was optimistic in his approach to man's condition on earth.

Accounts of Camara Laye's life differ, but we do know that *L'enfant noir* was published because a Parisian friend of the author read the manuscript and realized its significance. By the time he returned to Guinea, Laye was famous in France as a writer. He held a number of positions in the Guinean government, and presumably continued to write. Some time in the early 1960s, Sékou Touré, Guinea's president, learned of the new book that Laye was writing, presumably read the manuscript (or had someone read it for him) and decided that it was critical of his regime. Laye was given an ultimatum: he could remain in Guinea, but only if he did not publish the work.

Laye fled the country for Senegal and published *Dramouss* (a sequel to *L'enfant noir*) in Paris, in 1966, thirteen years after his previous book was published. The title of the English edition was *A Dream of Africa* (1968). The story begins as Fatoman (Laye) returns for a two-week vacation in Guinea after six years in France. The shocks that confront him are related to the ominous political changes in his beloved land and to his father's work status. Approaching independence, the country is torn asunder by quarrelling political factions and the final demands of the remaining *colons*. After a political rally, Fatoman refutes what the speakers have said and laments:

> Someone must say that though colonialism … was an evil thing for our country, the regime you are now introducing will be a catastrophe whose evil consequences will be felt for decades. Someone must speak out and say that a regime built on spilt blood through the activities of incendiaries of huts and houses is nothing but a regime of anarchy and dictatorship, a regime based on violence. (p. 146)

Moreover, describing a dream involving the goddess Dramouss to his father, Fatoman states of Guinea's future:

> I saw a people in rags and tatters, a people starving to death, a people who lived in an immense courtyard surrounded by a high wall, a wall as high as the sky. In that prison, force was the only law; or rather I should say, there was no law at all. The people were punished and sentenced without trial. It was terrible, because these people were the people of Guinea, the people of Africa! (pp. 183–4)

With the publication of *Dramouss/A Dream of Africa*, the mild-mannered writer had become, to quote Ken Saro-Wiwa, *l'homme engagé*.

On a more personal level, Camara Laye was equally disturbed by what had happened to his father during his absence. The artistry described so painstakingly in *L'enfant noir* had also been threatened by cultural upheaval. In order to make a living, Fatoman's father is forced to carve wooden objects for the tourist market, since the women who previously bought his delicate gold jewellery have become more interested in 'buying the junk imported by Lebanese and Syrian merchants' (p. 129). When Fatoman asks his father to give him the animal that he has been carving, his father tells him that the African goldsmith has become a thing of the past:

> In those days, the art of the blacksmith surpassed by far that of all other craftsmen: it was in all truth a noble art, a magician's art, a real art, indeed, which required more knowledge and more skill than the other arts. And so it was natural that in those days it was to the blacksmith one turned, not to sculpt a hind, something that anyone here can mock up, but to model the images of one's ancestors (and the most remote image of them all: the totem) to carve the masks for ritual dances, to fashion every cult object, which the blacksmith's inherent powers rendered sacramental by the very fact that it was he who created them. Though such powers have never entirely died out, my son, nevertheless I cannot conceal from you the sad fact that they have more or less lost their potency, and that it could hardly be otherwise considering the essential nature of our society which, although it did not break completely with its ancient beliefs, all the same allowed itself to be converted to Islam. If our caste is still a powerful caste, it seems to be by virtue of the fact that we blacksmiths and metal-workers are creating sculptures that are more and more remote from any kind of religious preoccupation. And it is not so much that the ideas of power and mystery have died, have disappeared, as that the mystery and the power are no longer to be found where they used to be; for they are beginning to fade away under the influence of modern ideas. That is why the hind you are going to take with you will never be anything more than an ornament, a decoration. (pp. 131–2)

The demise of his father's artistry may be understood as Laye's fear of the death of his own art.

The rest of his life was not easy, for Laye paid dearly for his decision to publish his third book. His works were banned in Guinea. Exiled in Senegal, Laye was provided with a research position at the Institute Fondamental d'Afrique Noir by the country's president, Léopold Sédar Senghor, with whom he shared an interest in literature and in *négritude*.[1] When Laye's wife returned briefly to Guinea because of a death in her family, Sékou Touré retaliated against the writer by placing her in prison, where she remained for seven years (Evenson and Beus, 'Camara Laye', 1997, p. 277). Laye's mental and physical health deteriorated, and he required intermittent periods of hospitalization. Though he published one further work shortly before his death – *Le maître de la parole* (1978), translated as *The Guardian of the Word* (1980), a retelling of the Malian epic, *Soundiata* – the remainder of his life was filled with abortive projects and abandoned manuscripts. One of these, a novel he referred to as *The Exiles*, might have shed light on his own predicament as a writer severed from his ancestral roots, but it was never completed.

When I met Laye in Dakar in 1973, he told me: 'No man is free to write what he wants in Africa today. No writer is free because African leaders are too sensitive – they won't listen to their poets, their artists, who in thinking are years ahead of the politicians' (interview with author, May 1973). One can't help noting the irony in the statement; Sékou Touré had reviled him, Léopold Sédar Senghor succored him. Laye knew that his very presence in Senegal might thwart a more positive dialogue between the two leaders, and this may have led him to abandon *The Exiles*, though apparently there was also the problem of writer's block.

Camara Laye was an unassuming man, a generous soul who infused his works with a rare vision of optimism and humanity. Though he described the role of the writer as that of a feeble man who takes the burden of his society upon his shoulders, those who met him encountered a person of great inner strength and fortitude. The title of his last published work, *The Guardian of the Word*, became his own obituary. The oral historian, the griot, he wrote in *Le maître de la parole*, should not be confused with hacks, 'those music merchants, those choristers or guitarists who wander through the big cities, looking for recording studios' (p. 24). Rather, the true guardian of the word, the griot,

one of the important members of that ancient, clearly-defined hier-

---

1. Laye is one of the few Francophone novelists who was genuinely influenced by the *négritude* poets and shared many of their beliefs.

archical society, is above all – preceding his status as an historian and consequently as the custodian of the historical tradition he teaches – is above all an artist, and, it follows, his chants, his epics and his legends are works of art. Therefore the oral tradition is more of an art than a science. And just as the African sculptor works, the griot does not represent historical reality in a matter-of-fact way; he re-counts it using archaic formulas; so the facts are transposed into entertaining legends for the ordinary man, but they have a secret meaning for those who can read between the lines. (p. 25)

Censorship

Apart from two or three specific countries south of the Sahara, the censorship of literary works in Africa has never been total. Instead it has been randomly directed at individual writers (sometimes individual works by those writers) who have offended figures in power. The issue has been one of politics. African leaders have typically been so thin-skinned as to tolerate little or no criticism from the press, if freedom of the press exists, which it often has not. Journalists have been the most vulnerable, but censorship of creative works, although egregious by western standards, has more typically been specific and sometimes even predictable. Thus, besides a swelling number of writers from South Africa and Malawi (Legson Kayira, Jack Mapanje, Lupenga Mphande, etc.), individual works by a host of other writers across the continent have been banned during the post-colonial years. The writers include William Saidi (Zimbabwe), Ngugi wa Thiong'o (Kenya), Nuruddin Farah (Somalia), Camara Laye (Guinea), Similih M. Cordor (Liberia) and René Philombe (Cameroon).

Once in a while a writer manages to bite back. In Chinua Achebe's fourth novel, the satirical *A Man of the People* (1966), Chief Nanga, the country's Minister of Culture, is more bush politician than refined aesthete, providing Achebe with an opportunity to poke fun at a number of incidents he may have experienced personally. Invited to the Minister's house, Odili (the narrator) makes a quick note of the books in the Minister's library: 'There was a decorative set of an American encyclopaedia, there was *She* by Rider Haggard, and also *Ayesha, or the Return of She*; then there were a few books by Marie Corelli and Bertha Clay – I remember in particular *The Sorrows of*

Satan. That was all really except for a few odds and ends like *Speeches: How to Make Them*' (p. 38). Worse, the Minister knows nothing about his country's own writers and doesn't mind admitting it. Odili notes: the 'Minister of Culture announced in public that he had never heard of his country's most famous novel and received applause – as indeed he received again later when he prophesied that before long our great country would produce great writers like Shakespeare, Dickens, Jane Austen, Bernard Shaw and – raising his eyes off the script – Michael West and Dudley Stamp' (p. 62). So much for being a writer in Africa.

The extremes of uncontrolled literary censorship are, one hopes, limited to the past. In South Africa during apartheid and in Malawi under Hastings Banda, the monster was unleashed and given free rein to devour almost anything in its path. Some of the South African examples appear more ludicrous than pragmatic: since separation of the races was to be achieved at any cost, the literary censors during apartheid even embargoed books that had nothing to do with racial mixing or glorification. Hence, at one time Anna Sewell's *Black Beauty* and Thomas Hardy's *Return of the Native* were banned because of the 'implications' of their titles. The absurdity of these examples was mind-boggling. At least the writers were deceased. But the net that caught so many South African writers, both of African and European descent, included individual works by internationally revered writers such as Nadine Gordimer and Athol Fugard, who wrote in English, and Afrikaners (the formulators and perpetuators of apartheid) who rocked the boat by daring to criticize their own heritage: André Brink, Etienne Leroux, J. M. Coetzee and Breyten Breytenbach.

Needless to say, the Censorship Board meticulously scrutinized the country's writers on the basis of race. As early as 1966, the *Government Gazette Extraordinary* announced a blanket banning of the works of forty-six black South African writers. Not a word they wrote was supposed to be published, reprinted or even quoted in the country. Writers who at that time, or later, found their entire oeuvre banned included Es'kia Mphahlele, Lewis Nkosi, Bessie Head, Can Themba, Richard Rive, Dennis Brutus, Alex La Guma and Peter Abrahams, to mention some of the most widely known. In some instances, these writers were banned because they were also Marxists and the South African authorities quickly discovered that reaction to their activities could be muted if they brought up the issue of communism. Saddest of all, literary careers were often abruptly truncated by the rigidity of the apartheid bureaucrats. Writers were permitted to leave the country but given exit permits that stipulated that they could not return (no return of the native). Ever. In London and in New York, groups of South African writers and artists, many drinking themselves into oblivion, wondered if apartheid would ever end without a bloody battle.

So many books and articles have been written about these banned writers that a few brief examples will suffice here. Bessie Head was driven to insanity by apartheid. A child of mixed parentage (her mother was white, her father black – an almost unspeakable combination for hard-line Afrikaners), she was abruptly reclassified from white to Coloured, and to a certain extent never recovered. Her masterpiece, *A Question of Power* (1973), thinly disguised the facts of her life as a child in South Africa as well as her subsequent years of exile in Botswana. If there was ever any proof needed of apartheid's psychological scars, Head's novel is that proof – banned, of course, in South Africa until the country's liberation in 1994.

Es'kia Mphahlele's *The Wanderers* (1971) describes the main character's inability to fit in anywhere else once exile from South Africa was imposed on him. The novel spans the geographies of West Africa, Europe and the United States (reflecting Dr Mphahlele's own wandering) in an attempt to answer the question: where does a South African belong? Although the book does not answer that question, Mphahlele himself did. He returned to South Africa before apartheid ended and was considered by some of his compatriots to have compromised himself, as if he was suggesting that apartheid might not be that bad after all. Yet, if he was not silenced by the government after his return to South Africa in 1977, Mphahlele effectively muzzled himself. However, there are others who, after Nelson Mandela became president, returned to their beloved land only to realize that their entire earlier careers had been built on attacking apartheid. Once the system was dead, there was little to write about.

The massive censorship, the excessive list of banned works in South Africa, included hundreds of individual writers from within the country, the entire publication lists of other writers, but also hundreds of other literary works from around the world that the country's censors believed threatened the apartheid system: the works of African American writers were typically banned (Richard Wright, James Baldwin, of course); white writers (Tennessee Williams, Ernest Hemingway, Robert Graves, John Updike, Robert Penn Warren, Kurt Vonnegut, Jean-Paul Sartre, Alberto Moravia, Carlos Fuentes, Nikos Kazantzakis, and dozens of others) for individual titles; African writers from other parts of the continent (too many to identify here). Under apartheid, there was no television for fear of what it would expose Africans to; and dozens – if not hundreds – of Western films were also censored, sometimes with the absurdity akin to the banning of *Black Beauty* and *Return of the Native*. In *The Apartheid Handbook* (second edition, 1986), Roger Omond provides the ludicrous example of the film version of Roger and Hammerstein's musical *The King and I*. 'In the 1950s and 1960s, for example, posters of *The King and I* were altered to show Deborah Kerr in the arms of a shadow. The original showed her being embraced by Yul Brynner playing the King of Siam: Siamese are Asians and the poster was thus thought to be contravening the Immorality Act' (p. 244), which prohibited the intermingling of races.

In near-by Malawi during the era of Hastings Kamuzu Banda, censorship of the country's writers was almost as extensive as that by South Africa's white minority government. Editors and publishers were required to submit their manuscripts to the Censorship Board before publication. According to James Gibbs, who taught at the University of Malawi from 1972 to 1978 and often directed plays for the theatre: 'In addition to having a play approved [before it could be performed] a license [had] to be obtained for every "theatre" and [a] repermit [had] to be obtained for each separate performance!' ('Experiences of Censorship and Theatre in Malawi', 1985, pp. 69–70). The Censorship Board routinely prohibited the performance of works such as *Waiting for Godot* and *The Good Woman of Setzuan*, as well as any play by Wole Soyinka who the censor believed had specifically maligned President Banda.

The censor deplored Gibbs's desire to produce African plays, while 'Shakespeare, Dickens and Tennyson were underperformed'. As Gibbs notes, the censor 'assured me that he approved of works of such writers without having to read them and he urged me particularly to produce *Treasure Island* which he had seen in Britain and thoroughly enjoyed!'('Of Kamuzu and Chameleons', 1982, p. 77). The real issue behind the censorship of drama, however, Gibbs says, was the cult of the President for Life, Kamuzuism:

> Malawi is a country in which the artist has no hope if he seeks to challenge the full might of the state and take on Kamuzuism slogan for slogan. For Malawi has her own national hero, who has established a national theatre of gigantic proportions in which he alone stars. The top-hatted hero grandly waves his fly-whisk to the thousands of women who dance before him and to the thousands of women who dance behind him and to the thousands of ministers and minions who dance attendance on him wherever he goes. Lines of flags (raised by convict labour in many cases) mark his progress and his softest word is picked up by microphones and blasted through dozens of loud-speakers and thousands of radio receivers. And woe unto him who ventures to lower the volume of one of them! The playwright cannot hope to contradict this Moving Shrine, this National Institution, this Slice of History. (p. 81)

Steve Chimombo, who remained in Malawi during Banda's years, to the chagrin of some of his compatriots, states:

> I was a perpetual target for government censorship in all its various forms, simply because I was, and still am, a playwright, poet, critic, fiction, and faction writer. I was the editor of a now-defunct academic journal and am still the editor of a new one on the arts. At each instance, I was the victim of the censors' curbs, manipulation, frustration, harassment of artists, and in my case writers' freedom of expression. The all-pervading presence of censorship meant that I ceased to create as a free agent since, right from the privacy of my room or office I had to battle with self-censorship: Will the Censorship Board allow this? How is it going to react to this statement, line, or paragraph? Sometimes, I even ended up short-circuiting myself, creativity just dried up, or if I wrote at all, the product had no hope of seeing the light of day in print. (('Thirty Years of Writing under Banda', 1996)

Chimombo further catalogues the many restrictions placed on writers, academics, journalists and others during Banda's time. Travel abroad was impossible without official approval. An elaborate informer network made people suspect even members of their own families. Letters were routinely opened and then – if permitted to be delivered – resealed with tape that bore the imprint 'Property of the Malawi Government'. Works that were once approved could subsequently be banned. Expatriates (mostly academics) could suddenly be deported, ordinary citizens were thrown into prison. A book on ecology called *The Green Revolution* was banned because of the last word in its title. Many of these same tactics existed in South Africa during apartheid, but Malawi's President was African.

Chimombo also notes that censorship begins with the writer himself/herself. Where the threat of censorship exists, it is the writer who makes the first cut: not including a scene in a novel or a play or a passage in a poem *before* it is written. My assumption is that many writers in countries where there has been no real pattern of official censorship have nevertheless censored their own works in the process of writing them. There are simply too many overly sensitive politicians and leaders to expect anything less. An earlier stage even before this includes works simply not written at all, for fear of recriminations by African leaders. The atmosphere in the Congo, Uganda, Sierra Leone, Liberia, Nigeria, the Sudan – nations which have had psychopaths as 'leaders' at one time or another – has not been conducive to any kind of creativity.

Assuming that a work has been written, then excision or alteration before publication becomes still another layer of censorship. We have already noted the willingness of some African publishers to submit creative works to governmental bureaucracies in order to guarantee that nothing is offensive or likely to prevent a book from being approved for the educational market. The issues here may not always be ideological but also religious and sexual. Still, they are genuine. Publishers outside the continent exert a different form of pre-publication censorship when they try to fit African writing into acceptable and anticipated patterns ('not African enough'; how many western writers have had their works rejected for not being western enough?).

One layer of censorship that exists in the United States – removing texts from local school systems, typically because of objections from conservative parents or school board members – appears not to have reached the shores of the African continent. However, a related form of censorship has existed for decades, going back to the colonial era, when religious schools controlled the materials in their often meagre libraries and purchased only those works that were deemed morally uplifting.

Thus, censorship in contemporary Africa often operates simultaneously on several different levels. How many hundreds of books by African writers have never made it into print?

Imprisonment

As often as not, censorship has gone in tandem with torture and imprisonment, or at least the threat of it. The case of Afrikaner writer, Breyten Breytenbach (see *The True Confessions of an Albino Terrorist* [1983]) chillingly demonstrates why many South African writers fled before they could be imprisoned. Extensive accounts of the torture of the country's political prisoners may have acted as a deterrent. Why stay at home and end up in prison when exile (with no chance of return) is an alternative? Once again, South Africa and Malawi have topped the list with the largest number of political prisoners, including creative writers.

One of the worst incidents involved Jack Mapanje, the Malawian poet, incarcerated for nearly four years. For three months, his cell was flooded with water up to his knees, making it impossible for him to sleep. Today, he still walks with difficulty. His poems in the volume titled *Skipping without Ropes* (1998) reflect on his imprisonment, though they are probably not as directly autobiographical as the account he is said to be writing. At a poetry reading at the Book Café in Harare during the 1998 Zimbabwe International Book Fair, Chenjerai Hove remarked of Mapanje's ordeal – a remark reflecting the lot of so many African writers – 'Most of us have terrible histories' (7 August 1998).

The imprisonment of African writers has been so frequent and widespread that it has led to an entire sub-genre. These are book-length accounts by writers (Wole Soyinka, Ngugi wa Thiong'o, Ken Saro-Wiwa) who have served time in their country's prisons; and novels, short stories and poems based on such experiences. The latter include Lewis Nkosi's *Mating Birds* (1986), Bessie Head's 'The Prisoner Who Wore Glasses' (1973), Wahome Mutahi's *Three Days on the Cross* (1991), Ken Saro-Wiwa's posthumously published *Lemona's Tale* (1996), and Dennis Brutus's volume of poems, *Letters to Martha* (1968). Other prison 'graduates' (to use Kwame Nkrumah's term) include Molefe Pheto, Kofi Awoonor, James Matthews, Todd Matshikiza, Micere Mugo, Percy Mtwa, Luís Bernardo Honwana and René Philombe.

One of the most disturbing cases of an African writer's imprisonment involved Wole Soyinka, from August 1967 until October 1969, recorded in one of his major works, *The Man Died* (1972). At the beginning of the Nigerian (Biafran) civil war, before his arrest, Soyinka published a letter in the Nigerian press, pointing out what he thought would be the futility of war. Critics of African literature have speculated that, at the outbreak of the Biafran War when the Ibos seceded from Nigeria, Soyinka may have been intellectually closer to the Ibos than to the Federalists who included his own Yoruba people. Early in August 1967, Soyinka made a hasty trip to Enugu to meet with Colonel Ojukwu, the secessionist leader, to try to prevent the imminent hostilities between the two groups. On 17 August, Soyinka was arrested in Ibadan. Two months later, Chief Anthony Enahoro, Federal Commissioner for Information, announced that Soyinka had confessed to helping the Biafran rebels both to purchase jets for the war and to help them overthrow the Federal government.

Soyinka denied the charges and was subsequently moved to a prison in Kaduna, in Northern Nigeria, where he was held until his release nearly two years later. He was never given a trial; there were rumors that he was ill and that he had died in prison. Most of the time he spent in solitary confinement. Denied writing materials, he wrote poems (published as *Poems from Prison*, in 1969) and *The Man Died* **between** the lines of print in books that were smuggled into his cell. One of the prison poems, 'Live Burial', begins as follows:

> Sixteen paces
> By twenty-three. They hold
> Siege against humanity
> And Truth
> Employing time to drill through to his sanity.

When Soyinka was finally released in October 1969, he took up a teaching position at Ibadan but soon afterwards left Nigeria and for a number of years worked on a variety of projects in Europe and the United States. In a brief comment at the beginning of *The Man Died*, published almost three years after his release, Soyinka states that his imprisonment involved 'the most rigorous security measures ever taken against any prisoner in the history of Nigerian prisons' (p. 8) and that he would not identify the people who aided him during his incarceration (some of them presumably still working as prison guards).

Soyinka provides his own explanation for why he was thrown into prison:

> My arrest and my framing were two entirely different affairs. The one was prompted by the following activities: my denunciation of the war in the Nigerian papers, my visit to the East, my attempt to recruit the country's intellectuals within and outside the country for a pressure group which would work for a total ban on the supply of arms to all parts of Nigeria; creating a third force which would utilize the ensuing military stalemate to repudiate and end both the secession of Biafra, and the genocide-consolidated dictatorship of the Army which made both secession and war inevitable.
>
> I was framed for my activities in gaol. I was framed and nearly successfully liquidated because of my activities inside prison. From Kiri-kiri I wrote and smuggled out a letter setting out the latest proof of the genocidal policies of the government of Gowon. It was betrayed to the guilty men; they sought to compound their treason by a murderous conspiracy. (p. 18)

Initially placed in jail in Ibadan and then in Lagos, Soyinka was moved to a maximum security prison in Kaduna, where he spent eighteen of the twenty-seven months. 'Detailed under emergency regulations' (p. 72), he was sometimes kept in chains but was aware of other prisoners and activities in the prison. He states that while still in Lagos there was a ban on all news from outside and that he 'had begun to lose sane distinction between the supposition and the reality' (p. 80). He lost all taste for food and water. 'Time vanished. I turned to stone' (p. 86). Some of the other prisoners in the Lagos prison were Ibos, whose crime was simply being Ibo at a time of rampant 'Ibophobia' (p. 111) within the country.

In Kaduna, where Soyinka was kept in solitary confinement, although denied writing materials, he could borrow books from the prison's so-called library, but after nine days he had read every title in the collection. He began to feel the loss of reality, as if he were being buried alive. It wasn't too long – in part perhaps because of frequent periods of fasting – before he suffered a series of hallucinations. Often he imagined that people he had known earlier in his life were in his cell, such as the poet Christopher Okgibo, who had died early in the civil war. Much of the time he was ill, from fever and complications with his eyesight. On one occasion when an Asian doctor was sent to observe him, Soyinka tricked the physician into looking at the ceiling and picked the man's pocket, thus gaining access to 'a cheap Biro' (p. 190).

The worst of his ordeal began during his second year in Kaduna, though it is difficult to tell to what extent his problems were exacerbated by fasting. On one occasion, Soyinka believed that Adolf Hitler was in his cell; on another, Albert Schweitzer. He wondered if he was pregnant because the shape of his torso changed so significantly: 'My pregnancy begins just below the navel, it is hard as stone, small and compact. It really looks as if I have secreted a large egg just under my skin. It is contradictory because the rest of my body is skin and bone' (p. 212). In a bizarre drawing he made of himself – reproduced in the text and described as 'Charcoal on toilet-paper' (p. 227) – he looks like a mad-man knotted in a yoga position. The drawing is consistent with the disgust he felt for his body.

Much of his time in prison was consumed with activities to keep his mind alert. From bits of string and paper, he constructed mobiles; he observed the lives and habits of insects and lizards with the attention of a trained scientist; he engaged in endless mathematical exercises ('Once I wrote out all the possible combinations of six digits' [p. 244];) on one occasion, he made a reed flute from a sunflower stalk, but the result was less than satisfactory. Above all, he listened to the sounds – any sounds of human activity – from the rest of the prison, sometimes aware that other prisoners were being tortured. For at least one period of his incarceration, he believed that he had conquered the problem of what to do with nothing. 'I had TIME! Often I woke up in the morning to a problem and one minute later, literally one minute later, the guard was tapping on the door to signal lock-up hour. I DESTROYED time' (p. 244).

In spite of all these 'diversions', the larger issue of *The Man Died* always remains Soyinka's slow death in prison, for it is the death of the mind that finally breaks the writer down. Soyinka's original title for the book was *A Slow Lynching* but, after reading a letter written by George Mangakis, a Greek professor imprisoned by 'fascist dictators' (p. 11), and learning the fate of one of his Nigerian compatriots who died of complications with gangrene ('The man died'), Soyinka decided to change the title of his own book. Nothing could be a more accurate statement of what had happened to him than 'the man died'. Such a belief is reiterated throughout the book. The demeaning situation for any prisoner is summed up in one brief sentence toward the end: '[A] prisoner is not a human being' (p. 279). Or if a human being, only for brief, fleeting moments.

One of those moments took place several months before Soyinka's release, when his wife was permitted to visit him. The prison authorities refurbished his cell, providing him with writing paper (an entire ream of 500 pages), pencils and pens, a typewriter, even carbon paper. And new books and journals, so new 'they seemed to have come straight from an oven round the corner' (p. 279). But it is the paper that excites him more than anything else:

How do I describe a clean, virgin sheet of typing paper? A tabloid of space, untouched, unmarked, without fold or wrinkle? What shall I term its equal that this sensation may be fully grasped? A spring? An oasis when hope is gone and the tongue is glued to its roots? As wine? No, not wine, not even wine after years of deprivation can compare with the smell and feel of a quarto sheet of paper in its inviolate purity. As a much junior sibling then who one loves dearly, loves to see in fine prints and little silver earrings, as a little sister dressed for communion, fragile and vulnerable, holier than the mother of Christ and more adorable. But it was not one sheet alone, it was hundreds. And there I sat, compelled to number them one after the other ... 50, 51, 52, 53, 54 ... 103, 104, 105 ... 207, 208, 209 ... It hurt. I wrote in the tiniest possible writing in the corner of the page. It was also stupid. This idea of numbering was to ensure that I did not use any of this paper for illegal messages. The officer stood over me while I performed this criminal philistinic chore. From 219 I moved backwards to 120, a slip that might seem natural enough if detected. It was not detected. At the end we attained the number 375. I asked him to report this figure to the Grand Seer because the packet did claim 500. I said, I didn't want to mention it until we checked, but did you notice the wrapping was torn? He had hardly left when I began to sort out the chunks which were twice numbered. I need not have hurried. The figure was accepted. (p. 278)

He need not have worried. 'One hour after she [his wife] had left the prison, a squad came in and swept out every item that had been given [him]. *Everything!*' (p. 280). Back to nothing. Yet he managed to write illegally, between the lines of the few books he was permitted, with the ballpoint pen snatched from the unsuspecting doctor. That was his sanity in the face of madness and what for a writer was the closest thing to death.

The years in prison broke more than Wole Soyinka's spirit. Yes, he became the first African writer to win the coveted Nobel Prize for literature (in 1986), but by that time and subsequently he had become an African wanderer, spending more time out of Nigeria than in the country. At the time General Abacha came to power – further undermining Nigeria's hopes for democracy – Soyinka had returned to teaching in Ibadan. Always outspoken, always the political activist, Soyinka had to flee the country or face Abacha's death squad. He left using an illegal passport, though Abacha subsequently placed a bounty on his head. Thus, even outside Nigeria, Soyinka had to be careful of his movements and live a life, at least temporarily, similar to that of Salman Rushdie.

After the civil war his creative energy turned towards the tragic, such as *Madmen and Specialists* (1971), and towards political commentary, such as *The Open Sore of a Continent*, mentioned earlier. Once known for both his tragic and his comic masterpieces (*The Lion and the Jewel* and *The Jero Plays*), as well as for any number of humorous poems, Soyinka has increasingly written about the darker aspects of his country's insanity. The old Soyinka died in that prison in Kaduna, in that sixteen- by twenty-three-pace cell.

Ngugi wa Thiong'o's incarceration in Kenya shares numerous parallels with Wole Soyinka's in Nigeria, but there are also significant differences. At midnight on 30 December 1977, the writer was arrested in his house at Limuru and the following day was taken to Kamiti Maximum Security Prison. The account of his imprisonment, *De-*

tained: A Writer's Prison Diary (1981), covers the year of his detention, ending on 12 December 1978, when he was released. Ngugi was not placed in solitary confinement but was able to communicate with other prisoners. Though ostensibly prohibited from writing, like Soyinka he wrote on toilet paper and scraps of paper given to him by prison officials. He had adequate reading materials, including occasional international news publications. Besides keeping notes on his imprisonment, he wrote *Devil on the Cross*, published in Gikuyu in Kenya in 1980, as well as a number of other works in his tribal tongue.

To a certain extent, it is language which got Ngugi into trouble in the first place. He was well known for his campaign for indigenous languages when he was chairman of the Department of English at the University of Nairobi. He regarded the use of English as a manifestation of neo-colonialism; he identified with the masses, particularly the working-class poor. Quite legitimately, it seems to me, he wanted Kenyans to be able to read literature in their own languages: 'Kenyan writers have no alternative but to return to the roots, return to the sources of their being in the rhythms of life and speech and languages of the Kenyan masses if they are to rise to the great challenge of recreating, in their poems, plays and novels, the epic grandeur of that history' (*Detained*, p. 196).

The event that triggered his arrest was a production of *Ngaahika Ndeenda* (*I Will Marry When I Want*) in Gikuyu 'by a group of workers and peasants from Limuru to a wide and very appreciative and most enthusiastic audience at Kamiriithu Community Education and Cultural Center' (pp. 174–5). What was his crime, he asks. 'For writing in a Kenyan language? For joining hands with peasants to build a modern patriotic Kenyan theatre? For communicating with at least a few peasants?' (p. 143). 'In my case, my unstated reasons for detention were my consistent opposition to the foreign control of our economy and culture, to the mental colonialism in the ruling comprador bourgeoise that makes them have a childlike faith in foreigners per se, especially if such foreigners happen to be British or American capitalists' (p. 147). Also, it could not have helped that earlier in the year (1977) Ngugi published *Petals of Blood*, an attack on neo-colonialism and multinational corporations, some of which were clearly attempting to curry favour with the Kenyan government.

More often than not, Ngugi saw himself as part of a wider, op-pressed group. Thus: 'A year as an inmate in Kamiti has taught me what should have been obvious: that the prison system is a repressive weapon in the hands of a ruling minority determined to ensure maximum security for its class dictatorship over the rest of the popu-lation' (p. 4). His own imprisonment 'is not a personal affair. It's part of a wider history of attempts to bring up the Kenyan people in a reactionary culture of silence and fear, and of the Kenyan people's fierce struggle against them to create a people's revolutionary culture of outspoken courage and patriotic heroism' (p. 28). Worse, 'Deten-tion without trial is part of that colonial experience of fear' (p. 44) which Kenyans in power, nearly two decades after independence, continue to inflict on their fellow countrymen. On the issue of language, here, too, the post-colonial attitude is simply an extension of the colonial position:

> The settler despised peasant languages which he termed vernacular, meaning the languages of slaves, and believed that the English lan-guage was holy. Their pupils carry this contempt a stage further: some of their early educational acts on receiving the flag were to ban African languages in schools and to elevate English as the medium of instruction from primary to secondary stages. In some schools, corporal punishment is meted out to those caught speaking their mother tongues; fines are extorted for similar offenses. Men at the top will fume in fury at fellow Africans who mispronounce English but will laugh with pride at their own inability to speak a single correct sentence in their own African languages. In some government depart-ments, the ability to speak the Queen's English, exactly like an upper-class English gentleman, is the sole criterion for employment and promotion. But since few, if any, Africans can speak the language exactly like those native to it, only Englishmen get employed or pro-moted to critical positions of authority. (p. 59)

In Ngugi's own case, then, language not only creates class distinctions, but also incarcerates.

Ngugi writes of the monotony of prison life, of medical com-plications for himself and other prisoners, of the stench of the prison itself, but his primary argument is that prison is a metaphor for colonialism. So little has changed for those in the penal colony, except that, in this writer's case, he sees more clearly, understands more fully, his situation in post-colonial Kenya (an oxymoron he would no doubt argue):

> In freedom, I used to see as through a film darkly; in prison I see in the clearer light of the 100–watt bulb in my cell that never lets me sleep; I see in the clearer light of the eyes of the keys-jangling guards who have completely stripped me of any privacy in eating, washing and shitting; I see it in the clearer light of the sickening nauseating food that I daily have to force down my throat; I see it in the clearer light of this Bleak House, this human zoo, where every hour I only look at stone and dust and iron bars, and more stone, dust and iron bars; I see it in the clearer light of the callous police use of disease as a means of torture; I see it in the clearer lights of the endless acts of humiliation meant to strip me of the last vestiges of humanness – like being chained as a condition for being treated in a hospital or being chained as a condition for seeing one's family; above all, I see it in the bright light of my certain knowledge and total conviction that the forces that pressed for and obtained my arrest and detention are the ones killing democracy and human freedom in this country. (p. 187)

When Jomo Kenyatta died, Ngugi and other inmates briefly hoped for a general amnesty which would release them from prison, but this did not happen. The greatest concern for the detained political prisoner – unlike ordinary convicted criminals with set terms – is how long incarceration will last, 'not knowing when one will get out' (p. 146). There is no time-frame that applies to the political prisoner, resulting in an intolerable situation. Ngugi found solace, however, in the prison writings of other Africans, particularly Wole Soyinka (there are direct references to The Man Died in Detained) and in Dennis Brutus's poems. But then one day, just as was true in Soyinka's case, he was released. There appeared to have been no logic to the timing.

Once on the outside after nearly a year in prison, Ngugi encountered a whole new set of problems, this time relating to his former position at the University of Nairobi. He was caught in another bind when he tried to return to the classroom: the university would not re-employ him, but he hadn't been sacked, nor had he resigned from his position. Letters to university officials were met with silence. Finally, at a meeting with the vice-chancellor, he was informed that his detention was an 'Act of State' (p. 209), which dissolved all earlier contractual relationships between him and the university, between Ngugi and the government. In short, the Act of State had made him a non-person, unemployable – a category not far removed from the 'stateless' status South African writers frequently discovered themselves in during apartheid. All that remained was departure from the country: exile.

Exile

Exile knows no return, or so the common belief has it, yet the variations of exile involving African writers have been so extensive that it is impossible to identify a single pattern. In the more than thirty years since the publication of his first novel, *The Beautyful Ones Are Not Yet Born* (1968), Ayi Kwei Armah has spent little time in the country of his birth, Ghana, though for most of those years he has lived in other African countries. Is he a writer in exile? Armah says no. Nor was he forced into leaving Ghana by events relating to his writing or the country's political situation. Where he lives (most recently in Senegal) has been his own choice, and presumably he can return to Ghana whenever he desires.

Is an African writer who lives outside the country of his birth but on the African continent living in exile? Were he alive today to answer the question, Camara Laye would no doubt answer in the affirmative, at least for his own situation. Laye was prohibited from returning to Guinea after Sékou Toré issued the ultimatum about his writing; he was also working on a novel called *The Exiles* before his death. Moreover, there is adequate evidence of his sense of estrangement from his native land, both during the earlier part of his life, as a student in France, and later when he sought refuge in Senegal. The other side of the exile issue applies to Nuruddin Farah who for decades could not return to Somalia. Living in other African countries, Farah has stated, does not place him in the category of exiled writer. Currently in South Africa, he is still at home, and, at the moment, it appears that there is no threat of reprisals if he returns to Somalia.

With South African writers during apartheid, with Ngugi wa Thiong'o, and certainly with a number of Nigerian writers while

General Abacha was in power, the question of exile becomes much more complicated. The one-way ticket into exile chosen by many South African writers before the end of apartheid so often resulted in neurosis, alcoholism and even madness that it is possible to argue that the South African government achieved exactly what it wanted: broken writers, silenced by their inability to continue writing. Only a few, such as Dennis Brutus, survived and continued to write productively. There is also the case of Es'kia Mphahlele who discovered that exile was intolerable and even with an exit visa stating no return – ever, if he was going to survive, he had to return to his native land.

Finally, there are all those other examples of temporary exile (though all exiles probably believe their condition is only temporary), that conclude with the triumphant return of the long-lost child, back to paradise (to use Nuruddin Farah's example). So Ghanaian Ama Ata Aidoo fled into exile in England for three years, until she no longer feared threats on her life. Jack Mapanje waits in England for the situation to improve in Malawi, even though Hastings Banda is no longer in power. Similih M. Cordor waits and waits in the United States, wondering if conditions in Liberia will ever make it possible for him to return home. The same is true of Syl Cheney-Coker in the United States, waiting for stability to return to Sierra Leone. Or Ngugi wa Thiong'o, still articulating Marxist rhetoric, while finding refuge in the capitalist West and apparently at ease with his situation.

> Exile has both positive and negative consequences. Negatively, a writer, any writer, needs the nourishment that comes from constant touch with the people about him he is writing [about]. It is even more important for one like me who is writing in an African language, Kikuyu, which is only spoken inside the country from which I have been exiled. Nothing can ever be an adequate substitute for that enrichment through contact. And now positively. One strives to make contact. One takes exile as a challenge. It can also make one see things to do with one's own country and history in a better perspective. (e-mail to author, 13 October 1998)

Or Wole Soyinka, who states that he has been in exile three times: the first following his imprisonment during the Biafran War, when he 'wrote' *The Man Died* in France (this was voluntary, but was certainly triggered by his imprisonment); a second time after the rigged 1983 election, when Soyinka was warned that a hit squad was out to get him [which was involuntary]; and, again, after General Abacha placed a bounty on his head because of inflammatory statements the writer made about the Abacha government. 'I was being turned into a non-person ... They would ... put me under house arrest and then from there make me disappear while they pretended I was under house arrest, they would take me somewhere else. We had details of how this thing was planned. And so, I decided it was time to move to go and establish the outposts of the resistance and let the world know exactly what was happening to our people' ('Soyinka Tells His Exile Story', 1998). Though he returned temporarily to Nigeria after Abacha's death, Soyinka waits patiently – a man of the world, in the United States and in Europe – to see whether Nigeria's move again to civilian rule will free his country of its horrendous military stranglehold. Even Chinua Achebe, who has taught in the United States for many years and was not forced to leave Nigeria, mused in a letter to me during the Abacha years whether it might be better to be back in the midst of everything, instead of thousands of miles away.

The fact is that many exiled writers, especially those who also hold academic appointments, have left their countries of origin because of better working conditions in the West. Ernest Emenyonu, a Nigerian, states that his exile and that of others is voluntary, because of political and economic conditions in the country of his birth: 'compelled by material circumstances to leave their home countries for sheer survival, and ... impelled by their consciences to seek respite for a while outside their countries' (letter to author, 7 October 1998). He describes himself as one of the last literary scholars to leave Nigeria. 'When situations change for the better, I suspect that the conscientious exiles will be the first to go back home. Others will rapidly follow.'

Others are not so optimistic, particularly when the exile has lasted many years. When confronted by Jerry Rawlings, the President of Ghana, on the question of the exile's return, Ali Mazuri (more an academic than a creative writer, though he has published one novel), identified a number of reasons why a permanent return to Africa, after having lived in the West for twenty-five years, is just about impossible. 'Migrating professionals,' as he described himself and other African academics living in the West, are subject to a 'pull-in force ... [that] involves better facilities, better pay, nicer working conditions and also greater freedom' ('Why "Exiles" Won't Come Home Soon', 1999). Mazuri responded to Rawlings' probings by stating that he originally left his teaching position at Makerere University in Uganda because of his fear of Idi Amin. But after so many years in the United States, his children do not think of themselves as Africans ('my kids are virtually Americans'). Worse, he told Rawlings, he believes that there was never any chance for his professional development in Kenya, the country of his birth. Yet he also admits a larger problem: 'The only reason we as Africans are not unified is that we have miserably failed to recognize diversity in a way that does not militate against an over-riding sense of nationhood in our respective countries.'

The one writer who appears to have adjusted most comfortably to his exile is Nuruddin Farah (born in 1945), who has spent almost all of his adult life outside Somalia, the country of his birth, beginning with his undergraduate studies in India, where he wrote his first novel in English, *From a Crooked Rib* (1970). Farah has lived and taught for extended periods of time in England, Italy, Denmark, the United States and several African countries (the Gambia, Nigeria and South Africa), yet, in spite of the years abroad, he is known as his country's major writer and one of the continent's most distinguished novelists (capped by the Neustadt Prize in 1997). All of his major writing, he states, has been undertaken outside Somalia. 'For me, distance distills; ideas become clearer and clearer and better worth pursing. I like to place an intellectual and a physical distance between myself and what I am writing' ('In Praise of Exile', 1990, p. 65).

Farah provides the example of sharing the galleys of his first novel with his family. His mother's reaction was an unsettling remark: 'But this [the situation involving the main character] happens every day, and Elba's life is as common as sandstorms in Mogadiscio' (p. 66). The remark taught him a lesson: the novel's magic for readers outside his country was not there for his mother. Perhaps he was writing for an international audience. A similar response from his own people had greeted Tutuola's *The Palm-Wine Drinkard* many years earlier.

Yet Farah confesses that all his novels are about states of exile in one way or another: 'about women shivering in a cruel, cold world ruled by men; about the commoner denied justice; about a torturer tortured by guilt, his own conscience; about a traitor betrayed' (p. 66). Distancing himself from the source of his material was *de rigueur*. 'To write a truly inspired work of fiction about Somalia, I had to leave the country ... Being away from home has provided me with the time to pursue my profession, that of a writer' (p. 67). In an equally revealing remark, when probed about his writing, Farah replied, 'I write because a theme has chosen me: the theme of Africa's upheaval and societal disorganization. And I write in order to recover my missing half' ('Why I Write', 1988, p. 1599). Perhaps more than others, Farah has learned to use his exile positively, to feed his writing in ways that his peers cannot.

The Death of Ken Saro-Wiwa

Kenule Beeson Saro-Wiwa's execution by hanging on 10 November 1995 was a travesty of justice, a mockery of human rights and a failure of international diplomacy. The shock-waves of his murder were felt around the world, especially in these troubled times when writers of the global South have had to flee into exile and go into hiding because of bounties placed on their heads, making one question whether the pen is mightier than the sword.

Writers rarely go gentle into that good night but Saro-Wiwa's murder will certainly go down in the records of totalitarianism as one of the most despicable. The inexperienced hangman brought in to do the job attempted to hang him five times before succeeding. Or was the difficult execution also part of the warning to others that even death at the hands of tyrants will not be swift and expeditious? Saro-Wiwa had spent the previous two years of his life being harassed and imprisoned by the Nigerian authorities because of his outspokenness about his people, the Ogonis, and the ecological destruction of their homelands by the international oil cartels, namely Shell Oil.

Before his death, Saro-Wiwa had become one of the most prolific and popular Nigerian writers in recent years, though his books, mostly self-published, were almost unknown and unavailable outside Nigeria. He had been a newspaper columnist for many years; he wrote and published works for the primary school market; and he wrote novels, poems and plays. Saro-Wiwa's most famous novel (and the only one in print in the West at the time of his death) is *Sozaboy*

(1985), based on his experiences during the Nigerian civil war. William Boyd, the English novelist who knew Saro-Wiwa well, has called *Sozaboy* 'a great antiwar novel, among the very best the twentieth century has produced' ('Introduction', p. ix). The novel's unforgettable opening sentence/paragraph dangles in mid-air, holding the reader breathlessly waiting for more: 'Although, everybody in Dukana was happy at first.' Thereafter, the story – in 'rotten English', as the author called it – describes a young man becoming a soldier, going off to fight, and hopefully returning home as a hero. Except that there is nothing to return to. Mene the soldier-boy returns to his village only to discover that, although he has survived, much of his village (including his mother and his wife) has not.

It isn't difficult to link the fate of Mene's villagers to that of the author's Ogoni people, though certainly when Saro-Wiwa wrote his masterpiece he had not yet gone through the radical change that would move him, like other writers from the continent, into the domain of social activism. There were other things he had to write first, including his enormously successful soap opera for Nigerian television, *Basi & Co*, which ran from 1985 to 1990 during the heyday of the oil boom. Saro-Wiwa wrote 150 episodes for the series and became enormously wealthy, in part because of the spin-off publications from the series.

It was after the Nigerian civil war that Saro-Wiwa became concerned about the plight of his Ogoni people, whose lands were the centre of the country's rich oil-fields. By 1980, only 1.5 per cent of the oil revenues found their way back to the Ogonis. Increasingly, as one military government followed another, the oil profits were pocketed by the country's military leaders or used for elaborate public projects in other parts of the country. Saro-Wiwa began to regard his people's plight as a form of 'domestic colonialism' (*A Month and a Day*, p. 73). The lands became an ecological disaster. The Ogoni people, he wrote, have (1) 'No representation whatsoever in ALL institutions of the Federal government of Nigeria', (2) 'No pipe-borne water', (3) 'No electricity', (4) 'No job opportunities for the citizens in Federal, state, public sector or private sector companies', and (5) 'No social or economic project of the Federal government' (p. 68).

As he observed what was happening to his people, Saro-Wiwa began publishing books with titles such as *Genocide in Nigeria: The*

Ogoni Tragedy (1992). Working with the Movement for the Survival of the Ogoni People (MOSOP) which he had helped organize, he made appeals to Greenpeace, Amnesty International and finally to the United Nations. Saro-Wiwa was carefully watched. It is surprising that he wasn't muzzled earlier, but until General Sani Abacha came to power, Nigeria had always had a free press. It wasn't until the Abacha government feared the possibility of Ogoni secession (a move that Saro-Wiwa had never suggested) that the writer/activist's days were numbered.

Saro-Wiwa's own account of his harassment by the Abacha government, *A Month and a Day* (published posthumously late in 1995), is an appalling picture of the Nigerian penal system. The narrative covers a year, beginning in 1993, though not the author's final imprisonment that would result in his execution. Ironically, Saro-Wiwa says that he had written a novel with a prison setting (*Lemona's Tale*, 1996), but nothing in his imagination had prepared him for the reality of incarceration. The details of prison life in *A Month and a Day* could hardly be more damning for any government. Saro-Wiwa describes being moved from prison to prison (like Wole Soyinka), being tortured mentally and physically, encountering prisoners as young as twelve who were often given no food except what was sent to them by families or friends. To survive in the Nigerian penal system, a prisoner had to have money; otherwise 'you were subjected to brutality and condemned to stand up all night to fan the guardroom bosses with old newspapers. If you had money, you might be allowed to stay outside the toilet room in which some of the inmates were forced to sleep, so cramped was the available space' (p. 40). Since Saro-Wiwa had plenty of money, he was able to survive. In almost surrealistic terms, he describes having to pay even for the meals of the security guards who moved him around the country (until he ended up in the Port Harcourt prison), of paying for doctors and the medicine they prescribed, since he – like Soyinka and Ngugi wa Thiong'o – suffered from acute medical problems.

The Port Harcourt prison, he notes, 'had been built in colonial times; it was, at that time, the largest prison in West Africa, and was well laid out ... but everything was in disrepair, everything was collapsing, everything was gone' (p. 224). There wasn't even a telephone for the prison officials to communicate with the outside world.

The infirmary 'was leaking like a sieve; there was no ceiling; the entire place was damp; there was only a bucket latrine; the narrow beds had rotten mattresses' (p. 226), but it was the safest part of the prison, which was jammed with 1200 inmates.

Somehow he survived. Eventually taken to court, he was given a 'six-count charge of sedition and unlawful assembly' (p. 219). Seemingly, the charges were intended as a warning, since he was released on 22 July 1993. As he remarks in his chilling conclusion: 'I had been detained for a month and a day, during which I had witnessed the efficiency of evil. In a country where virtually nothing worked, the security services, armed with all the gadgets of modern invention, made sure that all orders were carried out with military precision. And the men were marvelously faithful to their instructions' (pp. 237–8).

Days earlier, on 15 July, '132 Ogoni men, women and children, returning from their abode in the Cameroons, had been waylaid on the Andoni River by an armed gang and cruelly murdered, leaving but two women to make a report ... The genocide of the Ogoni had taken on a new dimension' (p. 238). The rest is a matter of public record. After the deaths of four pro-government Ogoni leaders (two of whom Saro-Wiwa had earlier regarded as sympathetic to his cause), Saro-Wiwa and eight others were arrested on 21 May 1994, and outrageously charged with their murders. Saro-Wiwa, a life-long pacifist, assumed that the four moderates had been killed by the government. In November 1995, after a military tribunal found the nine men guilty, Saro-Wiwa and the others were quickly executed. The trial was widely regarded as a fraud. Royal Dutch/Shell voiced public concern, but its words seemed hollow in light of the rapidly unfolding events.

Shortly after Saro-Wiwa's death, William Boyd summarized the implicit government attitude towards his deceased friend: 'He was a nuisance, someone who got in the way of rich men getting richer. So why not kill him?' ('Death of a Writer', 1995, p. 51). Coverage of the death in the *ANA Review* (the publication of the Association of Nigerian Authors, of which Saro-Wiwa was a past president) quoted Laure Ehonwa of the Civil Liberty Organisation, as stating, 'We are not convinced that the trial was free and fair because the standard of procedure did not guarantee the right of the accused' (Sola Olorunyomi, 'The New Hemlock', 1995, p. 23). The article further questions the reasons for trying Saro-Wiwa and the other accused men before a military tribunal instead of a civil court. 'The ANA in a statement signed by its president, Odia Ofeimun, said the sentence of Ken demonstrated the predictability of evil and injustice as the regular vernacular of life in our national affairs.'

Throughout his writing life, Ken Saro-Wiwa was not afraid to speak his mind, *l'homme engagé* in the face of government-sanctioned terror and repression. As the situation in Nigeria deteriorated in the 1990s and as the plight of the Ogoni people worsened, Saro-Wiwa used all his energy for the Ogoni cause, even though he knew he was risking his life. Nothing bothered him more than silence, which he regarded as complicity with repression. The plight of the Ogoni should have involved all men of conscience, not just the Ogonis themselves: 'The silence of Nigeria's social reformers, writers and legal men over the issue is deafening' (*A Month and a Day*, p. 64). One of the final statements of Saro-Wiwa's life, published in the Nigerian *Mail & Guardian* in May 1995, included the following prescient remarks:

A year has gone by since I was rudely roused from my bed and clamped into detention. Sixty-five days in chains, weeks of starvation, months of mental torture and, recently, the rides in a steaming, airless Black Maria to appear before a kangaroo court, dubbed a special military tribunal, where the proceedings leave no doubt that the judgment has been written in advance. And a sentence of death against which there is no appeal is a certainty.

Fearful odds? Hardly. The men who ordain and supervise this show of shame, this tragic charade, are frightened by the word, the power of ideas, the power of the pen; by the demands of social justice and the rights of man. Nor do they have a sense of history. They are so scared of the power of the word, that they do not read. And that is their funeral.

When, after years of writing, I decided to take the word to the streets to mobilise the Ogoni people, and empower them to protest against the devastation of their environment by Shell, and their denigration and dehumanisation by Nigeria's military dictators, I had no doubt where it could end. This knowledge has given me strength, courage and cheer – and psychological advantage over my tormentors ...

Whether I live or die is immaterial. It is enough to know that there are people who commit time, money and energy to fight this one evil among so many others predominating worldwide. If they do not succeed today, they will succeed tomorrow. We must keep on striving to make the world a better place for all of mankind – each one contributing his bit, in his or her own way. (pp. 1–2)

Ken Saro-Wiwa contributed more than his bit to bring about critical change in the country he loved. According to the western media, Sani Abacha, Saro-Wiwa's nemesis, died of a heart attack on 8 June 1998. The Nigerian on the street believes otherwise – that General Abacha was murdered in his sleep.

There is no question about the unfair burden of tribulations suffered by contemporary African writers. Worse, there appears to be no end in sight. When the Berlin Wall fell and the Cold War came to an end, writers in the Second World suddenly found themselves more advantageously positioned. As I write this, Salman Rushdie's fate does not appear to be as bleak as it has in the past, though obviously he still has to be careful. And even during the years of the *fatwa*, Rushdie continued to write and publish novels, suggesting that in one sense his creativity had not been silenced. This has not been the case for many African writers, who, cut off from their roots, have experienced a diminishing of their productivity and, even (during instances of forced exile), a complete silencing. When I edited *Under African Skies* (1997), an anthology of African short stories, one reviewer remarked that of the twenty-seven writers included in the anthology, nearly half had been imprisoned or forced into exile. No matter how their situations are interpreted, African writers have not found themselves on an equal playing field.

The Crisis in African Writing

In much of what has been known for 40 years as the Third World, book publishing today is in a state of despondency and frustration, and it is hard to find, in the lush pastures of the Euro-American book industry, anyone who cares. Cross-border publishing investment readily crosses the Atlantic in both directions, but does not venture southwards. Latin America, Africa and most of Asia still are seen primarily as export markets, and difficult ones at that. (Gordon Graham, *Publishers Weekly*, 15 February 1991)

The inflation-adjusted price of bestsellers has fallen dramatically since Adam Smith's *The Wealth of Nations* came out in 1776 at a cost that would amount to $615.38 today. Five hundred copies of *Wealth* were printed in the first run, and Smith was paid £500 – the equivalent of some $170,000 now. His take worked out to be the equivalent of nearly $350 per copy. (Peter Brimelow, *Forbes*, 9 March 1998)

§ THE crisis in African writing lies not with the writers themselves but in the complicated and debilitating environment in which they work. And yet, as anyone who has attended writers' workshops on the African continent has observed, they persist in their craft with an almost contagious determination to succeed; they keep on writing, even though many of them are never published. As demonstrated by the quality of the publications of the Baobab Press in Zimbabwe, talented young writers exist who are capable of forging a national literature if someone is there to support and publish them. In addition, there is a rich array of writers who have overcome near-impossible obstacles during the last half-century to create an extraordinary literature. That is the good news about African writing, The rest is not so simple.

Problems in the economies of too many countries constitute the foremost obstacle in the development of an audience of African readers for African writers. How ironic that thirty years ago, not long after the colonial era, books were more affordable than they are today. (True, the students I taught in Nigeria in the early 1960s were mostly children of affluent parents who could afford to send them to secondary school and to purchase the books required for their courses.) Students at Africa University in Zimbabwe, for all the university's admirable intention of creating a truly unique institution with a student body from across the continent, now find the cost of books prohibitive. How do students in a literature course develop any sense of what a novel (what a lengthy narrative) is if all they have read is an extract from the book? What will become of the next generation of African readers if books are denied to them because of high cost and the continent's dearth of libraries?

Students around the world are masters of getting around the system where the cost of books is involved. American students complain just as much as Africans that books cost too much, so they often make a copy of a book on one of the many copy machines in the library. But libraries in African schools rarely have copy machines available for their patrons. Moreover, for most American students the money saved by copying a book instead of purchasing it is so much additional pocket money for indulgences – money that is there in the first place, which is not the case with many African students. Or African readers in general.

In a recent issue of *Forbes*, Peter Brimelow calculates that before the industrial age books were luxury items affordable only by the rich. The advent of moveable type and mass production brought the price down dramatically. Moreover, the free flow of ideas produced by the availability of inexpensive books and periodicals has been central to the development of democratic societies – or at least of stable societies. Many African countries are today so strapped economically that the bookless society Hans Zell fears continues to thwart political and social change. As Gordon Graham writes in *Publishers Weekly*: 'Publishing does not flourish under dictatorships; freedom of expression is the flame that invariably ignites their downfall ... Bookless societies are dangerous to themselves and to the world.'

Bookless societies, readerless societies, authorless societies – what of the future if the transformations of the so-called information age bypass much of the African continent? Everyone loses, particularly because this is happening concurrently with a mass exodus of African intellectuals. Too many African writers today are refugees who have fled their societies because of the collapse of political stability. Others feel the need to be closer to where their readers are and, increasingly, this means not Africa but Europe or America. The brain drain of the continent's writers is one of the most disturbing aspects of the current situation.

So what can be done to improve the plight of the African writer, and particularly the next generation of writers?

Concerned individuals (particularly from the West) have been attempting to deal with this issue. Moreover, considerable amounts of money have been provided by international organizations (again, particularly from the West) to improve the situation of publishing on the continent. Again, how much more of this is necessary? How many more conferences must be held before the problems of publishing on the continent are rectified and the lives of African writers improved? More of the same, Hans Zell implies, will not significantly alter the current situation. If that were going to happen, it already would have. The days when African publishers were considered welfare cases must end.

At each Zimbabwe International Book Fair, solutions are proposed which would relax the economic stranglehold that grips most African publishers. Abolish taxes on paper for books and periodicals, and on imported books. Print inexpensive books (as the Onitsha pamphleteers have been doing for decades), especially for children in the lower grades (as the Indian government has been doing for years) to enhance both literacy and the climate for reading – particularly in the indigenous languages. Children who are avid readers and owners of books will become adults who are the same. But these solutions, however sensible, unfortunately depend on enlightened governments adopting national book policies and following them through and, in the past, international organizations willing to fund such projects.

A larger vision is necessary if anything is going to change substantially. In a speech, 'Culture, Memory, and Development', delivered to the World Bank in April 1992, Wole Soyinka proposed, as reparations for slavery, that African debt be abolished, a noble idea if there ever was one. He concluded: 'If the word "reparations" remains problematic, I suggest "annulment" – it has the attraction of echoing that "annunciation" of a new world order. Let all debts be, not forgiven but – simply annulled. Thus, we also *not* forgive, but annul the past. The twentieth century may thus be kindly recalled in future history as – The Century of Annulment? It is a worthy *fin de siècle* consideration, an ennobling project.' In an equally significant proposal for tackling part of the problem from the top down, Chinua Achebe in a subsequent speech, 'Africa Is People', at the World Bank (June 1998), made an impassioned plea for looking at all people in the same way:

> Africa believes in people, in cooperation with people. If the philosophical dictum of Descartes – I think, therefore I am – represents a European individualist ideal, the Bantu declaration – *umuntu ngumuntu ngabantu* (a human is human because of other humans) – represents an African communal aspiration.
>
> Our humanity is contingent on the humanity of our fellows. No person or group can be human alone. We rise above the animal together, or not at all. If we learned that lesson even this late in the day we would have taken a millennial step forward.

From the bottom up, there is the equally enlightened example of *Tsotso*, 'A Magazine of New Writing in Zimbabwe', published in Harare. I purchased a copy of this plain but serviceable literary magazine at the ZIBF in 1998. The cost? Two Zim dollars, equal to ten American cents at the exchange rates at the time. According to the editors, the goal of the publication is 'better reading and writing with every new issue'. In a discussion of the results of a questionnaire sent to the magazine's contributors, the editors of *Tsotso* note that '70% of the respondents submit that Zimbabwean writers have helped to change attitudes in Zimbabwean society by, among many reasons, focusing on women's issues, linking education to tradition, revealing the richness of Zimbabwean culture, tackling issues generally considered taboo, exposing injustices, and … jolting society out of its complacency.' The issue of *Tsotso* I purchased was No. 21, which is particularly encouraging given the short life of so many African periodicals. Although the magazine organizes writers' workshops, its most impressive attraction is its cost, less than that of a local newspaper, affordable for most readers.

There is increasing evidence around the continent of similar approaches to help new writers get into print and, just as important, receive the attention of other writers. Networking and workshops take place in many of the bookstores in the larger African cities. Zimbabwe, Ghana, Nigeria, Angola, South Africa, Lesotho, Swaziland, Mauritius and other countries have active writers' associations. Furthermore, there is the intriguing proposal by Gilbert Doho, a Cameroonian dramatist and novelist who writes in French, that a writers' co-op would be the most productive organizational framework for guaranteeing publication of serious work by committed writers. However, his suggestion that ten writers band together to form a co-op and contribute £50 each month, and that all production and distribution be shared by the members is limited, once again, by economic realities. Where are there writers who have disposable income of £50 a month? That figure can be reduced if the co-op is larger than ten writers and no member is given preference or power to force his material upon others. It's a good start for what might become a successful venture for writers in a given locale.

I should like to propose something more inclusive: a pan-African publishing house, funded by people and institutions both from Africa and the West, with an unpaid advisory board predominantly from the African continent. Crucial to the entire proposal is the belief that Africans should be in control of the publication of their own writers and that the degree of dependence on the West (both financial and editorial) be determined by Africans themselves.

The advisory board The advisory board should consist mainly of African members from as many areas of the continent as possible (but especially the Anglophone and Francophone ones), and a minority of international members drawn from people who have had extensive first-hand experience of working and living on the continent or an interest in African literature or experience in publishing. Doris Lessing, William Boyd and Toni Morrison immediately come to mind, though there are many others with obvious qualifications who are less-widely known. The advisory board would oversee all aspects of the institution itself, which should be incorporated as a non-profit foundation. It may be necessary for some international organization to fund the initial meeting(s) of the board but, in the true spirit of volunteerism, board members who are able to pay their own expenses should do so.

Fund-raising   Fund-raising is central to the success of the foundation. In the past, Africans have been on the receiving end of funding for publishing seminars, writers' workshops and publishing ventures. This has been part of the problem because it implies that someone from outside will always pick up the bill. I propose instead that donors be not only wealthy individuals and/or international organizations and corporations able to contribute significant sums, but also African corporations and individuals (especially writers), as well as Africans from the diaspora. No amount should be considered too small. Every donor would be listed alphabetically in the foundation's annual report, but *not* ranked by amount given. I hope that, on the annual report, African donors will predominate so that Africans have a sense that the foundation is theirs.

Selection of books   The actual selection of books for publication would be exclusively controlled by Africans, many of whom have first-hand publishing experience. A possibility for the early years would be some kind of continent-wide literary competition for one novel and one collection of poems to be published each year, chosen by the editorial board through blind submissions. Initial screening of manuscripts might be undertaken by local writers' organizations, regional committees or country committees, and their choices forwarded to the editorial board, which would make the final decision and prepare the manuscripts for publication. As much as possible, all of this work – at least until the foundation is fully established and profits are returned to it – should be done on a voluntary basis. As a matter of record, Chinua Achebe chose the first 100 books for the Heinemann African Writers Series, without remuneration.

Publication   The chosen volumes should be published simultaneously in as many African countries as possible (depending on the distribution network – see below), using the facilities of established publishing houses in those countries. A portion of the profit from each edition would be retained by the local publishing houses, but the books themselves should be modestly priced in order to attract the largest possible reading audience. Promotion copies should be provided for the media, especially review copies prior to publication – in order for the titles to benefit from advance publicity. Furthermore, a significant number of copies of each book should be donated to libraries, including school libraries. Libraries could aid the foundation by disseminating information about its goals. All the foundation's books should appear in both English and French editions, and shortly thereafter in indigenous languages when the readership has been established.

Distribution It is not necessary for books to be published in more than three or four countries if an adequate distribution network can be set up. Thus, a Southern African edition of a work might be printed in South Africa and distributed in Botswana, Namibia, Zimbabwe, Zambia and Malawi, with appropriate prices in the national currency printed on the cover. (Distribution over a wide geographical area assumes that many obstacles that currently exist are eliminated.) Above all, a major goal of the foundation should be that by guaranteeing the availability of their books in as many countries as possible, writers receive the greatest recognition for their work. At the moment, too much publishing in Africa is local. Yvonne Vera may be well-known in Zimbabwe, but she is scarcely read or even heard of in West Africa.

The writer For the writer, the major benefit of such a system would be visibility, especially if writers' organizations, libraries, the media and academic institutions are involved. It is not simply a matter of Yvonne Vera being virtually unknown in West Africa, as in the example above, but of, say, Ben Okri (for all his fame in the West) being hardly read in many areas of the African continent. Authors whose works are published by the foundation would receive combined royalties from the African editions of their work and, with proper attention paid to subsidiary rights outside Africa, significant royalties from other areas of the world. The goal is that a writer whose book is chosen for publication should be able to live for several years on the royalties from that work. Needless to say, the author's advance must be a significant amount of money.

The foundation itself As for the foundation itself, it must have its headquarters in Africa, perhaps on a rotating basis, or several offices in the major geographical regions of the continent. Above all, it should be regarded as an African enterprise, not as a western one. As time passes, the number of books published each year should be increased, and the involvement of new blood and additional people should be guaranteed. A distant goal should be the independence from any western involvement at all. Non-African members of the advisory board should gradually be replaced. Moreover, as profits increase, due to an increasingly strong backlist, economic input from the West can be curtailed. The model for the foundation might be similar to the economic challenge given to the Africa University in Zimbabwe: initially established by the United Methodist Church in the USA, the university has set deadlines for when church monies will be decreased and African money and control will be increased.

Secondary goals of the foundation might include the eventual establishment of individual publishing houses in African countries or closer links to those already in existence. The foundation might also establish a bilingual literary journal, priced inexpensively but produced in as attractive and professional a manner as possible. Links with several of the major African publications edited in the West (*Transition*, *Black Renaissance/Noir*, *Revue Noir* – journals with minuscule circulations) could result in wide readership of those publications on the African continent.

For nearly forty years I have been a privileged observer of the African literary scene, the beneficiary of my American birthright. If I hadn't taught in Nigeria in the early 1960s, I would not have read Amos Tutuola's *The Palm-Wine Drinkard* when I did, or Chinua Achebe's *Things Fall Apart*. I would not have been exposed to the Onitsha Market publications, available a few miles from where I lived, or have been able to purchase the first issues of *Black Orpheus* – one of the most exciting African literary journals ever published – as they began to appear at the Mbari Club in Ibadan; I would not have begun purchasing copies of the Heinemann African Writers Series as those titles appeared in West Africa or purchased that first edition of Achebe's *Arrow of God* in a CMS bookstore in Enugu not too long after it was published in England.

Privilege (American, white, middle-class) made all this possible. When I returned to the United States, the same privilege permitted me to search through American libraries and begin reading African writers from the rest of the continent, and to continue my graduate studies at Howard University and Indiana University, while simultaneously teaching and writing about the writers I was 'discovering'. (The discovery was mine alone; the Africans already knew they were there.) And what wonderful discoveries they were: the *négritude* poets, South Africa's anti-apartheid writers (many of whom had worked for *Drum*), and, shortly thereafter, the writers – Camara Laye, Similih M. Cordor, Atukwei Okai, Don Mattera, Wally Serote, Syl Cheney-Coker, Oswald Mtshali and many others – to whom I was introduced on a Fulbright short-term travel grant in 1973.

The privilege has continued, making it possible for me not only to correspond with other writers and meet with many African writers when they visit Washington, DC – where I have taught during most of these years – but also to observe Wole Soyinka's extraordinary achievement as both writer and director of *Death and the King's Horsemen* at the Kennedy Center in 1979, certainly one of the finest evenings I have ever spent in a theatre. Or to fly to Africa numerous times, or to attend the Zimbabwe International Book Fair. Or, when I need to locate any African publication from the most obscure book to the most inaccessible periodical, to be able to order it on inter-library loan and quickly have it in my own hands for a few weeks. Even inter-library loan is a service that I have come to take for granted, yet something (along with fax machines and e-mail) that professors at African universities generally do not have at their disposal. One hopes the Internet will eventually change all this, if and when electricity and telecommunications reach the level we take for granted in the West.

But there's the rub, *if and when*. What has been readily available to me has been denied to most African academics and scholars. A flight from West Africa to Harare in order to attend the Zimbabwe International Book Fair is so expensive that few Africans can afford the ticket, and their governments, these days, cannot duplicate the subsidies and perks that western academics have come to consider theirs by right. If only a handful of African writers can live on their royalties, what does that say about the possibility of attending a conference in Kampala, in Accra or in Cape Town?

African writers inhabit a world devoid of privilege or advantage, lacking in literate readers, adequate publishing outlets, and book buyers with disposable incomes. They also lack informed and understanding critics, and rarely encounter enlightened political leaders willing to acknowledge the importance of the arts. Writers are denied social and political stability, and their lives are threatened by censorship, forced exile, imprisonment and worse. And yet contemporary African writers have left an indelible mark on the continent's psyche as well as on the international literary scene. Those who say that nothing good has come out of Africa have not read the continent's writers. Without the opportunities available to their peers in the West or even in Latin America or Asia, contemporary African writers have none the less assumed not only the burden of the continent's humanity but have identified the pathway that will lead their compatriots beyond the present morass. The crisis in African writing is genuine but no larger than our lack of resolution in dealing with it.

Works Cited

Achebe, Chinua, *Arrow of God* (London: Heinemann, 1964).

— *A Man of the People* (New York: Anchor, 1967).

— *Morning Yet on Creation Day* (London: Heinemann, 1975).

— *The Trouble with Nigeria* (London: Heinemann, 1984).

— *Things Fall Apart* (New York: Anchor, 1994).

— 'Africa Is People', Presidential Fellow Lecture Series, World Bank, Washington, DC, 17 June 1998.

African Writers-Publishers Seminar (Arusha, Tanzania, 23–26 February 1998), Seminar Report (Uppsala: Dag Hammarskjöld Foundation, 1998).

Akinjogbin, I. Adeagbo, Letter, *West Africa*, 5 June 1954: 513.

Aremu, Tunde, 'A Pioneer, a Quiet Burial', *ALA Bulletin*, 24 (Autumn 1998): 9–10.

Armah, Ayi Kwei, *The Beautyful Ones Are Not Yet Born* (Boston: Houghton Mifflin, 1968).

— 'Larsony, or Fiction as Criticism of Fiction', *Asemka*, 4 (September 1976): 1–14.

Bâ, Mariama, *Une si longue lettre* (Dakar: Les Nouvelles Editions Africaines, 1980).

Bamhare, Miriam, 'Getting Hooked on Reading', Writers' Workshop, ZIBF, 5 August 1998.

Boyd, William, 'Introduction', to *Sozaboy* by Ken Saro-Wiwa (Essex: Longman, 1994): v–ix.

— Death of a Writer', *The New Yorker*, 27 November 1995: 51–5.

Breytenbach, Breyten, *The True Confessions of an Albino Terrorist* (New York: McGraw-Hill, 1986).

Brimelow, Peter, 'Why They Call It Harvard College', *Forbes*, 9 March 1998: 50–1.

Brutus, Dennis, *Letters to Martha* (London: Heinemann, 1968).

Calder-Marshall, Arthur, Revue of *The Palm-Wine Drinkard* by Amos Tutuola. *The Listener*, 13 November 1952: 819.

Chakava, Henry, *Publishing in Africa: One Man's Perspective* (Oxford: Bellagio Publishing Network, 1996).

— Talking Books: Henry Chakava in Conversation', *Bellagio Publishing Network Newsletter*, 21 (December 1997): 14–16.

— 'Children and Books: Kenya, a Decade of Publishing for Children (1988–1989)', ZIBF, 3 August 1998.

Chimombo, Steve, 'Thirty Year of Writing under Banda', unpublished essay, 1996.

Chirikure, Chirikure, *Hakurarwi* (Harare: Baobab, 1998).

Cordor, Similih M., *Modern West African Stories from Liberia* (Monrovia: Books for Africa Press, 1972).

— *Africa, from People to People* (Monrovia: Books for Africa Press, 1979).

— *New Voices from West Africa* (Monrovia: Books for Africa Press, 1980).

Conrad, Joseph, *Heart of Darkness* (New York: Dover, 1990).

Ekwensi, Cyprian, *When Love Whispers* (Onitsha: Tabansi, 1948).

— *Jagua Nana* (New York: Fawcett, 1969).

— *Jagua Nana's Daughter* (Ibadan: Spectrum, 1986).

Emenyonu, Ernest, *Cyprian Ekwensi* (London: Evans, 1974).

— 'In Memorium: Amos Tutuola', *ALA Bulletin*, 23 (Autumn 1997): 3–5.

Enahoro, Peter, *How to Be a Nigerian* (Ibadan: Spectrum, 1966).

Evenson, Brian and David Beus, 'Camara Laye', in Pushpa Naidu Parekh and Siga Fatima Jange (eds), *Postcolonial African Writers: A Bio-bibliographical Critical Sourcebook* (Westport, CT: Greenwood, 1997).

Ezenwa-Ohaeto, *Chinua Achebe: A Biography* (Bloomington: Indiana University Press, 1997).

Facts and Figures from ZIBF 98: Children (Harare: ZIBF, 1999).

Farah, Nuruddin, *From a Crooked Rib* (London: Heinemann, 1970).

— 'Why I Write', *Third World Quarterly*, 10 (October 1988), 4: 1591–9.

— 'In Praise of Exile', in John Glade (ed.), *Literature in Exile* (Chapel Hill: Duke University Press, 1990): 64–7.

George, Rosemary M., *The Politics of Home: Postcolonial Relocations and Twentieth-Century Fiction* (Cambridge: Cambridge University Press, 1996).

Gibbs, James, 'Of Kamuzu and Chameleons: Experiences of Censorship in Malawi', *Literary Half-Yearly*, 23, 2 (1982): 69–83.

— 'Experiences of Censorship and Theatre in Malawi', *Literary Half-Yearly*, 26, 2 (1985): 65–73.

Graham, Gordon, 'For Publishing, Crisis in the Third World', *Publishers Weekly*, 15 February 1991: S4.

Harding, M. Hassan, 'Beyond Upholding Tutuola's Dignity', *Daily Times*, 28 June 1978: 7.

Head, Bessie, *A Question of Power* (London: Davis-Poynter, 1973).

— 'The Prisoner Who Wore Glasses', in Charles R. Larson (ed.), *Under African Skies: Modern African Stories* (New York: Farrar, Straus and Giroux, 1997): 167–6.

Hill, Alan, *In Pursuit of Publishing* (London: John Murray, 1988).

Hove, Chenjerai, *Bones* (Harare: Baobab, 1988).

— Rainbows in the Dust (Harare: Baobab, 1998).

Ibagere, Eniwoke, 'In Once Literary Nigeria, "Things Fall Apart"', Washington Post, 3 February 1996: A14.

Ike, Chukwuemeke, 'Structures to Promote the Reading Culture in Nigeria', ZIBF, 3 August 1998.

Johnson, Babasola, Letter, West Africa, 10 April 1954: 322.

Kibera, Ngumi, The Grapevine Stories (Nairobi: Focus, 1997).

Kiriamiti, John, My Life in Crime (Nairobi: Spear Books, 1984).

Larrabee, Eric, 'Palm-Wine Drinkard Searches for a Tapster', revue of The Palm-Wine Drinkard by Amos Tutuola, The Reporter, 12 May 1953: 37–9.

Larson, Charles R., The Emergence of African Fiction (Bloomington: Indiana University Press, 1972).

— (ed.), Under African Skies: Modern African Stories (New York: Farrar, Straus and Giroux, 1997).

Lawal-Solarin, O. M., 'Books and Children', ZIBF, 1 August 1998.

Laye, Camara, The African Child (London: Fontana, 1959).

— A Dream of Africa (New York: Collier Books, 1971).

— The Radiance of the King (New York: Collier Books, 1971).

— The Guardian of the Word (London: Fontana, 1980).

Lindfors, Bernth, 'On Shocks, Sharks and Literary Archives', Daily Times, 15 July 1978: 34.

— 'Amos Tutuola's Search for a Publisher', Journal of Commonwealth Literature, 17 (1982): 90–106.

— 'Introduction', to The Wild Hunter in the Bush of Ghosts by Amos Tutuola (Washington, DC, Three Continents Press, 1982): xi–xvii.

— 'Postscript: Another Hunter's Tale', to The Wild Hunter in the Bush of Ghosts by Amos Tutuola (Washington, DC: Three Continents Press, 1982): 156–64.

— 'A "Proper Farewell" to Amos Tutuola', ALA Bulletin, 23 (Summer 1997): 4–10.

— (ed.) 'Introduction', Critical Perspectives on Amos Tutuola (Washington, DC: Three Continents, 1975): xiii–xiv.

Ling, Margaret. 'Response to Speakers and Notes on the Zimbabwe International Book Fair', ALA Conference, Chicago, 28 June 1998.

Mafundikwa, Ish, 'Yvonne Vera', Skyhost, 5, 3 (1997): 17.

Makotsi, Ruth L. and Lily K. Nyarika, Publishing and Book Trade in Kenya (Nairobi: East African Educational Publishers, 1997).

Mapanje, Jack, Skipping without Ropes (Newcastle upon Tyne: Bloodaxe, 1998).

Mazuri, Ali, 'Why "Exiles" Won't Come Home Soon', South African Book Development Trust/Zimbabwe International Book Fair. http:www. mediazw.com/zibf 2 March 1999.

Mbanga, Trish and Margaret Ling, 'An Aspiring Frankfurt Emerges in Africa', Logos, 4, 4 (1993): 209–14.

Moore, Gerald and Ulli Beier (eds), *The Penguin Book of Modern African Poetry*, 3rd edn (London: Penguin, 1984).

Moore, Bai T., *Murder in the Cassava Patch* (Monrovia: privately printed, 1968).

Mphahlele, Ezekiel (Es'kia), *The Wanderers* (New York: Macmillan, 1971).

Mungoshi, Charles, *The Milkman Doesn't Only Deliver Milk* (Harare: Baobab, 1998).

Mutahi, Wahome, *Three Days on the Cross* (Nairobi: Heinemann, 1991).

Ngugi wa Thiong'o, *Weep Not, Child* (London: Heinemann, 1964).

— *Petals of Blood* (New York: E. P. Dutton, 1978).

— *Detained: A Writer's Prison Diary* (London: Heinemann, 1981).

— *Devil on the Cross* (London: Heinemann, 1982).

— *Ngaahika Ndeenda/I Will Marry When I Want* (London: Heinemann, 1982).

— *Decolonising the Mind: The Politics of Language in African Literature* (London: James Currey, 1986).

— *Matigari* (Nairobi: East African Educational Publishers, 1987).

Nkosi, Lewis, *Mating Birds* (New York: St Martin's Press, 1986).

Nwoga, Donatus I., 'Onitsha Market Literature', *Transition*, 19 (1965): 26–7.

Nzeako, J. U. Tagbo, *Rose Darling in the Garden of Love* (Onitsha: Tabansi Bookshop, 1961).

Obiechina, Emmanuel, *An African Popular Literature: A Study of Onitsha Market Pamphlets* (Cambridge: Cambridge University Press, 1973).

Ogola, Margaret A., *The River and the Source* (Nairobi: Focus, 1994).

Ogunbiyi, Yemi, 'Tutuola in an Ocean of Sharks', *Daily Times*, 10 June 1978: 20.

Okri, Ben, *The Famished Road* (London: Jonathan Cape, 1991).

Okunoren, Segun, *A Gift to the Troubled Land* (Ibadan: Spectrum, 1991).

Olorunyomi, Sola, 'The New Hemlock', *ANA Review* (November 1995): 23.

Omond, Roger, *The Apartheid Handbook*, 2nd edn (New York: Penguin, 1986).

Onwuka, Wilfred, *The Life Story and Death of John Kennedy* (Onitsha: J.C. Brothers Bookshop, 1963).

Osikomaiya, Jide, 'Amos Tutuola – Victim of Exploitation', *Sunday Times*, 2 July 1978: 16–17.

Ouologuem, Yambo, *Bound to Violence* (New York: Harcourt Brace Jovanovich, 1968).

p'Bitek, Okot, *Song of Lawino* (Nairobi: East African Publishing House, 1966).

Peters, Lenrie, *The Second Round* (London: Heinemann, 1965).

'Portrait of Amos Tutuola', *West Africa* (1 May 1954). Reprinted in Bernth Lindfors (ed.), *Critical Perspectives on Amos Tutuola*: 35–8.

Pritchett, V. S., Revue of *The Palm-Wine Drinkard* and *My Life in the Bush of Ghosts* by Amos Tutuola, *New Statesman and Nation*, 6 March 1954: 291.

Robinson, Eric, Revue of *The Palm-Wine Drinkard* by Amos Tutuola, *West Africa*, 27 (February 1954): 179.

Rodman, Selden, Revue of *The Palm-Wine Drinkard* by Amos Tutuola, *New York Times Book Review*, 20 September 1953: 5.

Sallah, Tijan M. *Network 2000*, 4, 4 (Fall 1997): 4.

Samkange, Stanlake, *On Trial for My Country* (London: Heinemann, 1966).

Saro-Wiwa, Ken, *Genocide in Nigeria: The Ogoni Tragedy* (Port Harcourt: Saros Publishers, 1992).

— *Sozaboy* (Harlow: Longman, 1994).

— *A Month and a Day: A Detention Diary* (London: Penguin, 1995).

— *Lemona's Tale* (London: Penguin, 1996).

Sisulu, Elinor, *The Day Gogo Went to Vote* (Boston: Little, Brown, 1996).

Soyinka Wole, *Poems from Prison* (London: Rex Collings, 1969).

— *Madmen and Specialists* (London: Methuen, 1971).

— *The Man Died* (London: Rex Collings, 1972).

— *Collected Plays I and II* (London: Oxford University Press, 1973).

— *Ibadan – the Penkelemes Years* (London: Methuen, 1994).

— *The Open Sore of a Continent: A Personal Narrative of the Nigerian Crisis* (New York: Oxford University Press, 1996).

— 'Culture, Memory and Development', International Conference on Culture and Development in Africa, World Bank, Washington, DC, 2–3 April 1992.

— 'Interview: Nigeria Should Stick Together', *West Africa*, 18–24 July 1994: 1270–1.

— 'Soyinka Tells His Exile Story', News@FreeNigeria.org. 18 October 1998.

Speedy Eric (A. Onwudiwe), *Mabel the Sweet Honey* (Onitsha: Trinity Printing Press, n.d.).

Tadjo, Véronique, *Latérite* (Paris: Hatier, 1983).

— *A vol d'oiseau* (Paris: Fernand Nathan, 1989).

— *Le royaume aveugle* (Paris: L'Harmattan, 1992).

Thomas, Dylan, 'Blythe Spirits', *The Observer*, 6 July 1952: 7.

Tucker, Neely, Revue of *Under the Tongue* by Yvonne Vera, *WorldView* (Winter 1997–98): 78.

Tumusiime, James, 'A Decade of Publishing for Children in Uganda', ZIBF, 3 August 1998.

Tutuola, Amos, *The Palm-Wine Drinkard* (New York: Grove Press, 1953).

— *The Wild Hunter in the Bush of Ghosts* (Washington, DC: Three Continents Press, 1982).

— *Yoruba Tales* (Ibadan: Ibadan University Press, 1986).

Ude, A. O. *The Nigerian Bachelor's Guide* (Onitsha: Ude's Publishing Company, n.d.).

Vera, Yvonne, *Why Don't You Carve Other Animals* (Toronto: TSAR, 1992).

— *Under the Tongue* (Harare: Baobab, 1996).

— *Butterfly Burning* (Harare: Baobab, 1998).

West, Anthony, Revue of *The Palm-Wine Drinkard* by Amos Tutuola, *The New Yorker*, 5 December 1953: 206.

Williams, Lena, 'Celebrating Writers Who Defy All the Odds', *New York Times,* 22 October 1997: E1.

Woolf, Virginia, 'Modern Fiction', in *Collected Essays*, Vol. 2 (New York: Harcourt, Brace and World, 1967): 103–10.

Zell, Hans, 'Africa – the Neglected Continent', *Logos*, 1, 2 (1990): 19–27.

— 'Publishing: Books', *Encyclopedia of Africa South of the Sahara*, Vol. 3 (New York: Charles Scribner's Sons, 1997): 536–9.

— 'The Production and Marketing of African Books: A Msungu Perspective', *Logos*, 9, 2 (1998): 104–8.

Index